HEROIC PIGEONS

The sleek fighter planes of modern times are today's warriors with wings. While the electronic age has grounded the homing pigeon, the story of these undaunted couriers remains a part of our military history. Mission after mission these winged messengers have doggedly flown to their home base, sometimes responsible for the rescue of whole battalions.

Arch Whitehouse tells the story of the famous pigeon heroes — from GI Joe who saved the lives of 1,000 British troops at Colvi Vecchia to Cher Ami, famed World War I pigeon who rescued the Lost Battalion on October 4, 1918.

HEROIC
PIGEONS

by

Arch Whitehouse

G. P. PUTNAM'S SONS   NEW YORK

Books by Arch Whitehouse

WINGS OF ADVENTURE

HELL IN THE HEAVENS

HELL IN HELMETS

CRIME ON A CONVOY CARRIER

THE REAL BOOK OF AIRPLANES

FIGHTERS IN THE SKY

YEARS OF THE SKY KINGS

TANK: HISTORY OF ARMORED WARFARE

BOMBERS IN THE SKY

SUBS AND SUBMARINERS

YEARS OF THE WAR BIRDS

COMBAT IN THE SKY

ADVENTURE IN THE SKY

SQUADRONS OF THE SEA

BILLY MITCHELL

ACTION IN THE SKY

GENERAL JOHN J. PERSHING

LEGION OF THE LAFAYETTE

AMPHIBIOUS OPERATIONS

DECISIVE AIR BATTLES OF WORLD WAR ONE

EPICS AND LEGENDS OF WORLD WAR ONE

THE FLEDGLING — AN AUTOBIOGRAPHY

ESPIONAGE AND COUNTERESPIONAGE

SQUADRON FORTY-FOUR — A NOVEL

HEROIC PIGEONS

*To Boys and Girls
Everywhere*

ACKNOWLEDGMENTS

I am indebted to Mr. J. P. Hoffman, Information Officer, Headquarters, United States Signal Training Command of Fort Monmouth, New Jersey, who kindly furnished much up-to-date material and several photographs which appear in this book.

Mr. M. J. Alexander, Press Officer of the Air Ministry, Whitehall, London, was most co-operative in furnishing data and pertinent information on courier pigeons that were used in the British services in two world wars. Several official reports that had been made available to the British Broadcasting Corporation were also provided by the Directorate of Public Relations in London.

I also appreciate the details and training information found in the booklet *The Sport of Pigeon Racing*, published by the American Racing Pigeon Union.

Other material was drawn from the many military histories in my own library, but more important, in the development of this work, was the pleasure I gained from tracing the amazing histories of these gallant birds.

I can only hope the reader will enjoy their stories as much as I did in writing them.

CONTENTS

HEROIC PIGEONS

INTRODUCTION

This book is written to revive the little-known stories of hundreds of heroes on wings who in mission after mission braved heavy artillery fire, bursts of enemy machine-gun bullets, and the storms of inclement weather.

We have all thrilled to the gallantry of the Colonists who fought for our freedom in the Revolutionary War. The United States Marines have won great renown for their patriotism and sacrifices on half a hundred battle-fields. The Doughboys of World War I and the G.I.'s of a later conflict have all contributed chapters of valor to our nation's history. Our airmen, today's warriors with wings, have never failed to thrill us with their combats in the clouds and their great daring against heavy opposition while serving our country.

But there is another winged hero who is seldom mentioned, a feathered campaigner, who, unarmed, pits his sixteen ounces of weight and strength against the weapons of the enemy and seldom fails to carry out his mission. This winged messenger, the homing pigeon, is the most reliable member of any military service, a wartime courier who is always asked to perform astonishing feats of flight when all other means of communication have failed.

9

These brave little birds have completed their missions time and time again, staggering into their home lofts wounded and weary. Many have died on arrival, but each and every one has made history and honestly earned the decorations awarded to him.

Modern military operations rely completely on the lifelines of communications; once contact is lost between the fighting forces and the nerve center of operations, all high-level guidance is cut off. A battalion may be lost, friendly artillery may mistakenly shell its own forces, or communications from headquarters to the most vital sector of its front may be destroyed. When all wires are down, when all electronic systems have been put out of action, when soldier runners are unable to get through with an important message, there is one reliable courier left — the homing pigeon.

Today, the military program has been grounded by rapid advances of the electronic age, and a short time ago pigeons that were trained for the Army Signal Corps were honorably discharged and offered for sale. The pigeon-training courses and loft activities at Fort Monmouth, New Jersey, were closed down. Most of the 1,000 birds were sold to registered pigeon fanciers in all parts of the country — caretakers who could be relied on to give them care and affection for the rest of their days. Before the sale, however, the Army Signal Corps asked the Pigeon Fanciers Association to be ready for any future emergency that might require the service of these winged couriers. The birds were sold in lots of five pairs, with a minimum purchase of one lot and a maximum purchase of two lots.

Special provisions were made for fifteen pigeons whose actions had saved American lives during combat. The Army placed these World War II hero pigeons in eight public zoos and institutions throughout the country.

High on this list of heroes was "G-I Joe," who was credited with saving the lives of 1,000 British troops at Colvi Vecchia, Italy, during World War II. This carrier pigeon flew twenty miles in as many minutes, carrying an order to cancel the scheduled bombing of the village near the Volturno river. G-I Joe's action saved a British brigade that had entered the area ahead of the timetable.

"Yank" was renowned not only for carrying a message on the fall of Gafsa in Tunisia, but also for covering 90 miles in 100 minutes to carry an urgent message for General George Patton, Jr.

"Caesar" was entrusted with 44 combat messages in North Africa, and on one occasion he flew 300 miles to deliver important information, crossing the Mediterranean to his own loft in Tunisia.

Pigeons had been used by American forces as early as 1870, when a number of them were employed by the old 5th Infantry in the Dakota Territory. Some pigeons went along with General John J. Pershing's troops on the punitive expedition to Mexico, and by the time the United States entered World War I these birds had proved to be so worthy that more than 20,000 were acquired, 5,000 of which went overseas to France. In this campaign the

best remembered is the famed "Cher Ami," who saved
the Lost Battalion on October 4, 1918. This brave little
bird, whose full story will be related later, was awarded
the French Croix de Guerre (War Medal). "Cher Ami,"
now suitably mounted, can still be seen at the Smithsonian
Institution in Washington, D.C.

During World War II about 40,000 racing pigeons
were voluntarily supplied by civilian fanciers to the Army
Signal Corps. Once they were fully trained, many of these
birds were used in about twenty campaigns, proving to be
most valuable in forwarding information gathered in action behind enemy lines.

During the European invasion through France into
Germany, 134 United States Army birds were signed on
for the Roer (Rur) river crossing, and during this advance 25 important messages and 67 map overlays were
carried by them.

Pigeon communications proved most effective with
small ships, as well as in jungle and mountain terrain in
the Southwest Pacific area. A loft was established behind
enemy lines in Burma, and pigeons were put to use by
agents as well as by forward troops.

And thus came the end of an era. These gallant little
birds were given good homes and creature comforts, but
the chronicle of their deeds will long remain a glorious
page in our military history.

1 · · · How It All Began

The homing pigeon, as we know him, is a direct descendant of the dove — sometimes called a wood pigeon — which probably originated in Europe, although the species known as the passenger pigeon was a North American bird that was found in thousands in the backwoods of Kentucky, Ohio, and Indiana. But the passenger pigeon was hunted so ruthlessly by the hungry pioneers of the early days that the species is now extinct. The domesticated homing pigeon was probably brought to this country by British immigrants, and these birds, in turn, stem from a common ancestor known as the Blue Rock pigeon. The so-called carrier pigeon is not in the same class as the homer, since he seems to be a breed that has been produced for his show plumage rather than for practical purposes.

The European homer was domesticated many years ago, and there is a record of pigeons being kept as pets or for poultry supplies as early as the Fifth Egyptian dynasty, or about 3000 B.C. Pigeons were used as postal messengers in 1150 by the Sultan of Baghdad, but this novel communications system broke down when Baghdad fell to the Mongols in 1258. So pigeons have been employed as messengers for more than 800 years.

The most detailed records of these feathered messengers being used in war operations can be found in the history of the French Revolution of 1848, when they were trained to carry dispatches from Paris to French and Belgian newspapers beyond the battle area. Pigeons also carried messages over areas that were not covered by the early telegraph lines of that era.

Pigeon racing and the development of the homing pigeon must be credited to the Belgians, who staged 100-mile races as early as 1818. Under the auspices of the *Société Colombophile*, Belgium's pigeon-racing organization, a contest was flown between Paris and Liège in 1820, and three years later a memorable race was staged between London and Brussels. By this time nearly every village in Belgium had its own pigeon club, and today the annual feature is the *Concours National*, a 500-mile race between Toulouse and Brussels.

The sport was also taken up by many Britishers, and by 1881 they were holding important meets and races between well-known cities of the British Isles.

All these early incidents are interesting and have left their mark on history, but we cannot forget that long before these dovelike birds were enlisted into military operations, another pigeon, possibly the best-remembered courier and often described as a dove, was released by Noah from the Ark. When this bird flew back toward evening of that day with an olive leaf in its beak, Noah knew that the flood was subsiding, that he would find land, and that life could go on again.

In olden days the soldiers of Rome, recognized the value of pigeons as war messengers. When Julius Caesar was staging his war against Gaul, he used courier pigeons to keep the public up to date on the day-by-day progress of his campaigns. A dispatch was prepared and tied about the neck of the daily courier. On the bird's arrival the original report was copied and the extra messages were flown to other towns by relay fliers.

The Olympic Games were also publicized through the use of homing pigeons, and sport fans of the era used to stand around for hours awaiting the arrival of the news of the various events. As soon as each competition had been completed the result was rushed off by pigeon courier, and this news was excitedly read by citizens in faraway towns just as baseball fans in this country await the play-by-play reports of the World Series.

The homing pigeon was perhaps first employed as a regular military courier almost half a century before Christ was born. Marcus Junius Brutus, noted Roman politician, it will be remembered, sided with Pompey the Great during the Roman civil war. At one time in this campaign, Brutus was trapped in the old city of Modena by Mark Anthony, who had dug deep, broad trenches around the city and strung a series of anti-shipping nets to prevent boats or small ships from using these channels.

Friends of Brutus made frantic attempts to get important messages and information to him; and divers, carrying thin sheets of lead on which the information was engraved, were ordered to try to work their way under the nets. Mark Anthony's sentinels soon caught on to this trick and the message-carriers were speared whenever they appeared on the surface.

At a critical point, someone remembered that civilians deserting Modena had carried baskets of domesticated pigeons with them. It was the obvious thing to make military couriers of them. Short messages were tied around their necks and the birds were released. Obeying their instincts, they flew back home with these military dispatches. This idea worked out so well that in a short time Brutus received important information and certain tactical plans that enabled him to sever the blockade.

A fabulous story of the value of these winged couriers will be found in the history of the Dutch city of Leyden. In 1574 the Spaniards held the city under siege and the unfortunate people were at the mercy of these invaders for months. During that dreadful time hundreds of people died of starvation, but even worse, cholera, then known as the Black Plague, killed thousands more. As brave as the Dutch people were, hunger began to betray them, and they were forced to kill their pet dogs and cats for food.

On one occasion, when taunted by their oppressors,

they set up a message on the city walls which read: *"We will never give in. So long as you can hear a dog bark or a cat mew, you can be sure we will hold out!"*

But the stocks of grain and domestic animals could not last forever, and finally parents could no longer look on the hunger-parched faces of their children.

"Please give in," they begged the city officials. "No oppression by the Spaniards can be any worse than watching our children starve to death."

But the officials refused, and the population began to riot. Some of the enraged citizens set fire to a number of public buildings. Others marched on the town hall and threatened the burgomaster. "Surrender and save our children," they screamed, "or we will kill you!"

The burgomaster went into executive session while the mob seethed outside. For a time it looked as though they were about to break down the doors of the great building. Refuse material was gathered to start more fires, but still the city officials held out.

Suddenly someone looked up into the sky and pointed. A pigeon was seen flying in from out over the sea. The little bird crossed the great sea wall, circled the town, and then headed for his home pigeon loft.

Tied to his tail feathers was a message from the Dutch admiral, a great naval hero admired and trusted by everyone. The message was read aloud from the steps of the town hall and the whole population cheered. The church bells were rung and the screams of rage of the people

turned into cheers of joy. The Dutch fleet was on its way bringing food, medicines, and fresh troops to replace the exhausted soldiers.

Outside, the enemy was most perplexed for they had no idea what had caused this new jubilation and the increased defiance, but with the ringing of the church bells they sensed that victory had somehow been snatched from their grasp.

One wonders what might have happened had that pigeon faltered in his trust, had he taken the wrong course or joined other birds on a food-foraging mission. He might have arrived too late to save the town and the brave people of Leyden.

Carrier pigeons have long played important roles in man's commercial communications. During the twelfth century, the Sultan of Baghdad set up a most efficient pigeon-post service that was the envy of his neighbors. These birds flew thousands of letters, written on silk paper, to every prominent city of the Sultan's empire. This system became so important that a chain of watchtowers was erected along the main route, and watchmen, on duty day and night, kept track of the birds, checked the arrival of each one, and provided feed and care.

A historic financial stroke has long been credited to a homing pigeon that was used in the banking network of the famed Rothschild family. It is generally believed that the family's fortune was started by a message flown in by a homing pigeon — a message that brought the result of the battle of Waterloo to London hours ahead of all routine communications of that day. This story is not true but the incident is worth telling, if only to refute the long-held legend.

In winning the Battle of Waterloo, Great Britain became the foremost European power, and advance knowledge of this battle's outcome resulted in a multimillion-dollar scoop for Nathan Rothschild, who was handling the British base of the family operations. When the Rothschild brothers left their Frankfort home in Germany to set up their financial network in various cities in Europe, they sent out endless items of commercial interest and in time developed a private news service in which homing pigeons had an important part. All this news was of vital importance to them in their dealing in the world's stock markets.

The outcome at Waterloo was of great interest to all professional investors, and for days during that fateful 1815 conflict the London Stock Exchange breathlessly awaited the news. If Napoleon was victorious, British stocks and consols (British government securities) would drop in price. If Wellington won, French exchange values would fall and Napoleon's empire would crumble.

The fate of Europe was shrouded in the smoke of battle for more than thirty hours. Then, late in the afternoon of June 19, a man named Rothworth, who was an agent for the Rothschilds, hurried to a boat at Ostend. He carried a Dutch newspaper that was still smudged with printer's ink. Early the next morning Nathan Rothschild stood at Folkestone harbor awaiting his agent. It took but a minute to scan the news, then hurry back to London, thereby beating Wellington's military envoy by several hours. Nathan Rothschild went into the London Stock Exchange, and there, instead of buying up all available British consols, sold every one he owned.

This shrewd move gave the impression that Nathan Rothschild had advance information as to the result at Waterloo, and everyone else began to sell the British securities. Then, when their value had reached absolute bottom, Rothschild suddenly bought a tremendous parcel for almost nothing. Moments later, when the news broke that Wellington had been victorious at Waterloo, the price of British consols soared to new heights. It was possibly the greatest financial stroke in the history of the Rothschild family fortune.

Baron Paul Reuter was a noted German communications expert, a newsman who quickly adopted Samuel Morse's electric telegraph. In 1849 he set up a line running from Berlin to Aix-la-Chapelle over which he telegraphed his news. However, there was a critical gap between Brussels and Aix-la-Chapelle, a gap that held up his despatches. To overcome this, Reuter set up a pigeon-post system over this unconnected area and each news item was written in triplicate and carried by three different birds, released a few minutes apart. This homing-pigeon system was so reliable that not only were mechanical failures overcome but more than eight hours were saved in the delivery of each telegram.

The Franco-Prussian War of 1870 saw pigeon communications reach a high degree of reliability, and the accomplishments of these little birds were brought to the notice of military planners in many countries.

In this war the Germans soon overwhelmed the French and quickly set siege to their beloved city of Paris. The City of Light was completely ringed in by the enemy for four months. Famine threatened. This was one of the coldest winters in French memory. Great trees in the famous parks had to be felled to provide fuel and heat. Old pictures show great bonfires being built in the poorer sections, around which people huddled to keep warm.

But although the people of Paris were besieged, they were undaunted and continued to keep in touch with their friends outside. They manufactured balloons in the armories and railroad stations, inflated them with gas, and sent them off at night in front of friendly winds to carry messages and general news. In some instances important officials were flown over the heads of the besieging forces.

The success of these silent vehicles of the air created a new idea, and the pigeon-fanciers of the city gathered in all available homing birds — about 300 — and shipped them out by balloon to friends in the south of France, an area not occupied by the enemy. The art of microphotography had recently become the rage in Paris, and tiny letters, mottoes, verses from the Bible, and other classical writings had been transposed to small discs and set in rings and lockets. Thus the happy combination of pigeon and microphotography provided the besieged French with a new means of vital communication. Messages of length could be placed on very small sheets of paper, and the pigeons, whose home lofts were in Paris, would instinctively head there once they were released. In these instances the messages were inserted in small tubes that were fastened to the pigeons' legs.

But first a complete microphotography outfit, as well as the pigeons, had to be shipped outside. The operation was to be made by two balloons. One was named *Daguerre* for Louis Daguerre, the French inventor of the daguerreotype (a photograph produced on silver, or a silvered plate treated with iodine vapor) and the second balloon was named *Niepce* in honor of J. N. Niepce, who had perfected an early form of the photographic film.

Daguerre and *Niepce*, one bearing the baskets of birds and the other the microphotography equipment, were released. Shortly after leaving the ground, *Daguerre,* which was carrying the photographic equipment, was shot down by the German artillery. On seeing this the crew aboard *Niepce* quickly jettisoned all extra baggage and rose to a higher level. They floated about for nine days, weaving back and forth over the enemy lines until they were able at last to bring *Niepce* to earth near the city of Tours, 129 miles southwest of Paris. All the birds arrived in good condition, as they had been well fed and tended during the long aerial voyage.

When *Daguerre* was shot down, another microphotography set was soon assembled and, along with another balloon, loaded on two farm carts with the idea of secreting them out of the city. When the wagoners tried to drive out of Paris, the wagon that was carrying the balloon was captured by enemy sentries. The driver of the second cart evaded the German guards, however, and eventually transferred the microphotography equipment to old wine barrels and, playing the role of a wine peddler, reached Tours safely.

A postal system from Tours to Paris was established and the birds, bearing letters and military orders, flew regularly over this long route. The system was enlarged in time and much mail from England was transposed to microfilm and forwarded to Paris. The average letter was reproduced on a sheet about the size of a postage stamp, inserted into a section of a goose quill, and tied to the pigeon's tail feathers with a silk thread. On delivery in Paris the message was magnified by a special projector, thrown on a screen, copied by a postal clerk, and delivered in a standard, readable form.

The Tours-to-Paris pigeon post was expensive for businessmen who had to use the facility. For instance, a film that bore fifty letters of about 20,000 words would cost the senders 1,000 francs — about $250 in American money. All this money went into the French Post Office funds. On one occasion an unnamed pigeon carried eighteen films, bearing about 40,000 messages — a trip that brought in more than $50,000 to the Post Office.

A comparable system was employed by the United States Government during World War II when soldiers' letters were transposed to reels of microfilm and reproduced later on a sensitized form for delivery. This saved considerable cargo space at a time when ocean shipping was needed for more important war supplies.

Another intriguing feature of this early balloon-pigeon system was the fact that it provided the first aerial battle in history. Felix Nadar, writer and balloonist, met an enemy sentinel balloon at an altitude of 10,000 feet while trying to navigate a balloon from Tours to Paris. A German soldier in the basket of the enemy gasbag opened fire, but Nadar, who had expected such an emergency, "shot his way out of the predicament," and landed safely in Paris.

It is curious to note that this early German balloon corps was trained by Henry Tracy Coxwell, an English surgeon-dentist who was a noted aeronaut of that day.

Toward the end of the siege the Germans devised a plan to stop the pigeon post. They rounded up a flock of trained hawks and turned them loose every time a pigeon was seen heading in or out of Paris. In order to overcome the "hawk fighter" opposition, the French used an old Chinese device, in which bamboo whistles were fitted to the homing pigeons' tails. As they swept through the air on their missions, their slipstream provided the "wind" that blew the whistles, a weird noise that frightened off the hawks. These antihawk whistles were still used by United States Army pigeons until the end of World War II.

Courier pigeons employed in the Franco-Prussian War set up a brilliant record considering that they had not been trained to work under war conditions and fly through the worst part of a bitter winter. Many in fact were beaten down by the weather, some were shot down by enemy gunfire, and others were destroyed by hawks before the protective whistles could be provided. The fact remains that the couriers that did fight their way through are said to have delivered 100,000 official military messages and more than one million letters to private citizens.

2 · · · Training and Care

The training of racing pigeons, or homing pigeons as they are termed by today's fanciers, has been developed over the long years of their domestication. The pigeons developed for military courier work are a simple variation of the racing pigeon, a bird bred and trained to fly from one point to another in competition with other birds belonging to owners who are associated in these sporting events.

All homing pigeons, except a selected few that are reserved for breeding, are placed in the training program from about the time they are twenty-eight days of age. They are taught to enter the loft through a trap and to exercise above and around the loft, and gradually they are taken away for short distances in wicker baskets and released, upon which they are expected to find their way home in the shortest possible time.

A few years ago a group of French pigeon fanciers mapped out a test flight to see if one of these birds could fly over 7,000 miles from Arras, France, to his home in Saigon, Vietnam (then Indochina). The pigeon selected was young, in the pink of condition, with clean, glossy feathers and firm muscles. His mother and father were swift racers but more important, he was a very intelligent bird of proven courage and endurance.

This gray homer was shipped from his loft in Saigon in a covered basket and stowed aboard the dark hold of a ship that took weeks to sail through the Red Sea and the Mediterranean until it reached France. Throughout the voyage the bird had no opportunity to see land of any sort, and could not have memorized any particular landmark or details of the shoreline. On his arrival in Arras he was fed and cared for and given a chance to recover from his confinement. Then, amid a cheering throng of people, he was tossed aloft, and twenty-five days later he checked in at his home cote in Saigon. He had lost just over an ounce in weight after covering the 7200 miles, but appeared none the worse for wear.

Training and good care are most important in the development of the birds for racing. They should have clean drinking water and a good diet of seeds, cereal grains, green foods, and grit, all of which should be clean, sound, and of good natural color. The loft is usually built on an elevated site so that it can be seen from a good distance. The aviary section is well roofed, and is covered on at least

two sides with suitable poultry wire mesh. Perches and
nest boxes are set in sheltered sections, but the loft proper,
which bears the trap on the roof, accommodates the simple
mechanism required for accepting the returning birds and
the timing mechanism by which their arrivals are registered.

In their training flights, or in actual races, the birds are
taken to prearranged distant points by train, truck, or
automobile and there released to find their way back to
their own lofts. In an actual race each bird is banded with
a rubber countermark by the secretary of the association.
This is used in final identification and in computing the
pigeon's speed in yards-per-minute. In other words, although all pigeons in the race are usually drawn from one
area, there always must be a difference in the distance
from the release point to the birds' individual lofts. These
differences are not more than a mile or so, but to make the
competition fair their efforts are calculated in yards-per-
minute, rather than by the actual time taken to fly from
the release point to the home loft.

Once the birds are liberated, their owners, who are
standing by at the home lofts, anxiously watch the sky for
the return of their entries. Since time is of the essence, the
speed with which the birds can be induced to enter the loft
trap may make the difference between gaining a "win" or
a second place. As soon as the returning pigeon enters the
trap, his rubber countermark is removed from his leg and
inserted in a special capsule, which is then dropped into a
slot in the top of a special timing clock. With this, a crank

is turned which records the exact second the bird has clocked in.

Knowing the time of the bird's liberation, the race secretary, who later breaks the seal and reads the tape, calculates the exact number of seconds against the actual distance flown. This gives the pigeon's speed in yards-per-minute.

The sealed clock is then returned to the club offices, where the times of arrival of all birds are compared and the winners of the race are determined. Modern-day races include flights of 1,000, 1,500, and even 2,000 miles.

Training pigeons for military operations requires much the same program, but in addition the birds have to be taught to return to mobile lofts that are erected on trucks or trailers, and encouraged to fly while carrying special capsules for messages that may be fastened to their legs or fitted to their backs.

The racing pigeon became such an important feature of our defense arm that it was ordained a breach of the federal law, as well as the laws of many states, for any person, other than the owner, to maim, kill, or have in his possession any properly banded racing pigeon. The game departments of many states are still constantly alert to arrest and punish anyone who breaks this law. They also report to their owners or to the National Pigeon Union any lost, crippled, or dead racing pigeons they find within their jurisdiction.

As soon as a newly hatched pigeon is a week old it is

marked with a seamless aluminum band that is slipped over its foot. In a few days the foot will have grown so large the marker cannot be removed. Stamped in raised letters on each band is a notation, such as, AU-63-CIR-926. The "AU" indicates the American Racing Pigeon Union, the national organization; the "63" is the year the pigeon is banded; "CIR" represents the initials of the club to which the owner of the pigeon belongs; and "926" is the serial number of the pigeon. No two bands carry the same serial number, and once a band goes on a younger bird it has a permanent identifying mark that it carries all its life.

Army birds, according to information provided by Fort Monmouth officials, were banded by the Signal Corps. They usually carried two identifying markers, one on the right leg bearing the letters "U.S.A." to show they were the property of and trained by the U.S. Army. On the left leg the band may have carried U.S.A.-59-FtM-234, indicating that this Army bird had been hatched in 1959 at Fort Monmouth, New Jersey, and that his identifying number was 234.

We return to the question of how a homing pigeon is able to locate his home no matter how far away he is taken. This type of bird was first brought into Belgium from Asia in 1818, and careful study reveals that it is a mixture of almost two hundred varieties, all descended from the wild Rock pigeon. Belgian fanciers spent many years breeding this new strain for distance racing. The modern homer has been crossed with the French Smerle — which is actually related to the owl — the French

Cumulet that is capable of high-level flights, and the husky British Dragoon pigeon. The present-day bird is sturdy and graceful, with widespread wings for long flights. The breastbone is deep and powerfully muscled. The wing feathers are so important that if one is broken the bird's flight is greatly hampered, and if a tail feather is pulled out the bird will have difficulty in maintaining a steady course. The average homing pigeon weighs about one pound, but a cock bird may be two ounces more.

An old Arabic legend explains why the feet of a homing pigeon are always red. When the dove (actually a pigeon) returned to Noah's ark, it was noticed that she had a splash of red mud on her feet. This was so cheering to Noah, who had seen nothing but water for forty days, that he made a thank offering and prayed: "May pigeons' feet always be red."

The head of a homing pigeon is comparatively small, but his brain is one quarter larger than that of the ordinary pigeon. He is very intelligent and will persevere to the point of stubbornness; some have been known to fly a hundred miles off course to avoid a storm.

A story coming out of Fort Bliss well expresses the loyalty of the homing pigeon. Sent out on a training flight, one of these birds by mistake landed at a private fancier's loft. This unregistered owner, to keep the bird near his own home until he had become adjusted to the new surroundings, clipped his wings. Days passed, and when the pigeon did not appear, Fort Bliss officials gave him up. But imagine their amazement when one day, the clipped-wing bird finally reported in. He had *walked* all the way!

Another pigeon that failed to return after a message flight also reported in weeks later — walking. It turned out that he had alighted for water and his wing feathers had become covered with sticky oil so that he could not fly; he marched home, a distance of nearly ten miles, and delivered his message to the back door of the loft. He was unable to scramble up to the trap board.

Some pigeon experts claim that this bird is gifted with a form of built-in radar that helps him to find his own loft after hours of flight, for hidden under his head feathers are two very sensitive ears, while his sharp, prominent eyes can see great distances in daytime. It is doubtful that they can see at all at night. An interesting feature of their eyes is a transparent film that can be flipped from side to side like a windshield wiper, and protects them from sandstorms, smoke, and sharp winds.

The homing pigeon's ability to fly from dawn to dark, covering from fifty to seventy miles every hour, can perhaps be credited to nine air sacs under his ribs and certain empty spaces around his heart and lungs. The air sacs are filled with warm air in case his lungs need an extra supply during a rugged trip, and the air spaces add natural buoyancy that enables him to stay in the air with comparative ease.

Why do homing pigeons fly home? They are not unique in this inherent skill; it is found in most migratory birds, in bees, ants, toads, and even turtles, which have been known to travel hundreds of miles to return to their

A loft attendant inspects the wingspread of a homing pigeon. The speed and maneuverability of a pigeon is influenced by the condition of his feathers.

homes. But in the animal world, the homing pigeon alone can be trusted with his freedom, and trained to carry out the missions that men demand.

Experts who have made a serious study of homing pigeons have of late reached the conclusion that homers who successfully cover great distances — such as the bird which flew from Arras to Saigon — appear to find their way by means of the system of tiny canals hidden within their inner ears. This delicate network seems to be attuned to the magnetic rays that have existed for more than three million years in the air, sea, and earth, although our scientists are just becoming aware of them.

That is to say, this built-in homing device is in some way comparable to the mechanical instrument used by aviators when flying blind, but the pigeon's personal instrument is less complicated and far more efficient than that devised for men to use when they fly. Thus, when homers are first released they will circle the liberation area, apparently getting their bearings, but most likely tuning in on the electric impulses that will lead them home.

Some skeptics argue that the homing pigeon has no basic instinct to return to his loft, but that the natural urges of hunger and his longing for the company of his mates builds up an almost human desire to be at home with his friends. However, interesting experiments have been made with pigeons near radio stations where, once released, the birds appear to become confused because the radio waves cross the magnetic waves and interfere with them just as an electric storm interferes with a home radio set. The United States Navy once held trial flights at Oceangate, New Jersey, with two groups of pigeons that were to fly to their lofts at Lakehurst about ten miles away. The first group was released while a short-wave transmitter was being operated nearby, and this group took fifty minutes to cover the short ten miles. The second group, which was liberated while the transmitter was shut down, arrived in Lakehurst in less than twenty minutes.

Again, in tests conducted at Youngstown, Ohio, near Station WKBN during a sunny morning that was perfect for flying, one group of birds that was released while the station was silent flew straight home to its loft. A few minutes later when WKBN went on the air, the pigeons were seen to flutter about aimlessly and finally scatter in every direction. In another test, made in Paris, birds were released from the roof of a well-known broadcasting station. Here the radiation was very strong; the birds refused to fly and settled on the ground, just as they would when encountering an electrical storm.

3 · · · A Classic Adventure

M odern-day pigeon adventures began with World War I when, for the first time, immediate news of war action was made available to the general public a few hours after it had happened. Previous to this time, the outcome of battles fought hundreds of miles away, was seldom known for days. Individual exploits had to wait for some free-lance correspondent to write them and hope that his stories would be published months later.

The Great War of 1914–18 changed all this. For one thing, the bulk of the war was fought in western Europe, and its activities, victories, and defeats could be transmitted in a matter of minutes by telegraph and the new wireless systems. Hundreds of periodicals were hungry for the news: every scrap of it was published soon after the event, and gobbled up by thousands of readers everywhere.

One of the more memorable of these adventures occurred in May 1917, when a British flying boat, H.12-8666, took off from the Great Yarmouth station on the east coast of England. No pigeons were involved in the opening of this remarkable aerial adventure, but one, in particular, saved the day and several lives in the latter part of it.

This particular flying boat was armed with three Lewis guns and carried four 100-pound bombs that were intended for enemy installations along the Belgian coast line. The pilot was Flight Sub-Lieutenant Robert Leckie, a Scottish-born Canadian. His navigator was Flight-Lieutenant Galpin. Chief Petty Officer V. F. Watling was the radio operator, and Air Mechanic O. H. Laycock acted as the flight engineer.

These four men had actually planned a rather risky patrol, a decision that always adds zest to any game, but on this flight they had no idea what was in store for them. As soon as they had flown out about eight miles, Leckie decided he would send out no more radio messages, chiefly to prevent the enemy's sensing his presence in this area.

As they cruised along at about 6,000 feet, searching the waters below for traces of enemy submarines or surface patrol vessels, they were amazed and delighted to spot a German Zeppelin less than ten miles away. Leckie immediately dumped three of his four bombs to lighten the aircraft, and thereby gain speed and altitude, in the hope of attacking the big dirigible.

He gradually gained about 2,000 feet and was slightly above the enemy gasbag, and in a short time he was within two miles of it. The grim clouds probably formed a backdrop that screened them from the Zeppelin crewmen, because they made no effort to get away. Not until Leckie was almost on them did they dump their water ballast and attempt to ascend rapidly.

Making the most of his height, Leckie dived on the big dirigible, and Galpin, who was in the bow, began to fire into the enemy gondola. Incendiary ammunition pierced the silver envelope. Then one of Galpin's guns jammed, and the other failed with the next burst. The flying boat was now roaring alongside the Zeppelin as the German crewmen drenched it with gunfire from the big aluminum gondolas.

Leckie darted about, hoping Galpin could clear one of the gun stoppages, but before this was done a red glow appeared in the airship's middle. The British flying boat had to turn away as the glow increased and a huge fire swept upward. The Zeppelin L.22 went up in flames, then twisted down, a bundle of metal wreckage, and plunged into the sea.

For the first time a cumbersome old flying boat, with luck and the courage of its crew had downed a majestic Zeppelin. The news was flashed around the world in a very short time, and the crewmen were suitably decorated for this amazing performance.

Flying boat 8666 was now world-renowned and she continued her routine service in the war, but the following September she played a new and even more glamorous role. In this adventure a land plane, a British D.H.4, took off to attack two enemy airships reported off Terschelling Island of North Holland. This two-seater aircraft was much faster and more maneuverable than the flying boat and, in addition, was better armed for engagements with dirigibles. It did not have floats of any kind although it regularly carried out missions of six hours or more over the North Sea. This type of aircraft was being used on a temporary basis until a more suitable machine could be put into production.

On these offensive patrols the land planes were usually escorted by H.12 flying boats that might conceivably support the D.H.4's in any action. But, more important, in the event of an emergency the flying boats could act as rescue ships.

Thus, the D.H.4, accompanied by Number 8666 with Flight-Lieutenant Leckie again at the controls, cruised toward Terschelling Island. Squadron Commander Nicholl was in actual command of the flying boat; Air Mechanic Thompson was radio man, and Air Mechanic Walker acted as engineer officer. The D.H.4 was flown by Lieutenant Gilligan, and Lieutenant Trewin was his observer-gunner.

The twosome flew toward enemy territory for nearly ninety minutes by which time they had reached Terschelling Island with the flying boat cruising at 12,000 feet, but the land plane was held at the 9,000-foot level. At noon the D.H.4 crew received a message by signal lamp from the flying-boat commander that read, "Climb as high as possible and attack Zeppelins."

This message was a surprise to Gilligan and Trewin, who had not observed anything resembling a Zeppelin.

They signaled back, "Fine, but where are these Zeppelins?"

The answer came swiftly. "Dead ahead! Close in and attack!"

It turned out that two Zeppelins, L.46 and L.44, were only a few miles away and were just turning about to make for their base of operations at Borkum, a German island in the North Sea. The D.H.4 made a brave effort to climb and get to where the big dirigibles were cruising along. Gilligan hoped to get above L.44 and dive on her, but the Zeppelin commander was dropping ballast fast and his airship was rising like an express elevator. Commander Nicholl, aboard 8666, which had retained its 12,000-foot level, fired a few rounds but without effect.

But Nicholl stuck to his task and stalked L.44 for about an hour, or until the Zeppelins had enticed the two airplanes over two German light cruisers. Meanwhile the D.H.4 was having trouble with its engine and could not gain the required height, but Gilligan continued to stalk his prey and fire whenever an opportunity arose. But luck was not with the British planes; nothing they could do seemed to have any effect on the German gasbags.

Suddenly disaster struck: Gilligan's engine stopped cold, and nothing he could do would get it to twirl again. His position was serious, for he was miles from home over enemy waters with German cruisers, destroyers, and minesweepers spread out below. Gilligan signaled his trouble to Commander Nicholl, who simply answered, "Follow me and try to make Yarmouth."

The D.H.4 crew received the message with a grim snort,

for by then they realized that their radiator had been pierced by a bullet and that the engine had seized up. Their only chance was to get down safely onto that white-crested water, in the hope that Leckie could pick them up with his flying boat. Gilligan did not know that 8666 was also experiencing engine trouble. Enemy fire had damaged a magneto and only one bank of cylinders was firing on one engine. If he dared to go down into that sea, the pilot would need every ounce of power he could raise to get off again.

Fortunately, the D.H.4 pilot knew none of this; he was too engrossed in getting his plane down reasonably intact. He remarked later, "A heavy sea was running and I knew I had to take a wild chance. I started a pancake landing from about seventy feet up and we hit with a horrid crash. I had hoped to dab down as lightly as possible, but the next thing I knew I was well down in blue water. Even worse, I couldn't seem to free myself to scramble to the surface. I tried everything. I inflated my life jacket and then I remembered that my headphones were still attached to the panel. It was this stout cord that was holding me down. The instant I disconnected it, I shot to the surface like a cork. Then I saw Trewin swimming toward the wreckage of our machine."

The instant they realized that the land plane had crashed, Nicholl and Leckie went to the rescue. They knew that their own power was running low, that enemy vessels were in the neighborhood, that their radio equipment had been shot out of action, and that they had no food — a far from pleasant situation, but they did not hesitate for one moment.

Number 8666 was put into such a steep dive that she went into a sloppy spin for a minute, and Leckie just managed to pull her out in time to escape the same pile-up that had finished the D.H.4. Gilligan and Trewin swam toward the flying boat and in a few minutes were hanging on to the sides of the hull. Trewin was almost exhausted and had to be hauled aboard by the radio man and the engineer, but Gilligan scrambled in by himself.

All well and good, but now there were six men aboard 8666 instead of four, and power was falling off badly. They could only hope to taxi home on the surface of the rough sea, and possibly to be picked up by a friendly craft.

"If we could only get a message through to Yarmouth," Leckie started to say, and then remembered that 8666 was carrying a small basket that held four homing pigeons. He had never found it necessary to use these couriers before. "If we can get a message through to Yarmouth," he began again, "they'll put out an alert and we should be picked up within a few hours."

"There's no assurance this hull will hold together that long, the way the seas are running," Nicholl muttered.

Thompson, the radio man, had been instructed how to write a message on special paper and insert it in the leg tube of the pigeon, and Nicholl made up a report that read:

H.12N.8666. We have landed to pick up D.H.4 crew

about 50 east-by-north of Yarmouth. Sea too rough to
get off. Will you please send for us as soon as possible
as the boat is leaking? We are taxiing west-by-south.
V. Nicholl.

The first pigeon was sent off with this message and fortunately got through. There is no record of the names or
identifications of any of these birds, but one of them
played a most heroic role before this air-sea drama ended.
One of the four birds that were sent off was not heard
from again.

After they had drifted for forty-six hours, Nicholl sent
out another message:

3.P.M. Very urgent. Seaplane 8666 to C.O. Air Station, Great Yarmouth. We have sighted nothing. Wind
has been drifting us W.N.W. since we landed, so we
may have missed Cromer. We are not far from coast,
as we keep seeing small land birds. Sea is still rough.
Machine intact. We will fire Very (signal) lights every
45 minutes tonight. V. Nicholl.

Nicholl made two copies of this message and sent them
off with two birds, but one of these birds was found dead
the following morning some miles from the station.

In the meantime the Great Yarmouth station had sent
out many types of patrol vessels and aircraft to search for
the two missing planes, but by nightfall there was no trace
of either. Destroyers, drifters, motor launches, and trawl-

ers had gone out, but darkness fell and the seamen took a brief rest and awaited the dawn. Early the next morning every available aircraft went out but found nothing.

About ten o'clock on Friday morning an exhausted pigeon, true to his trust, reached Great Yarmouth with a copy of the second message. On arrival he floundered into his cote, fell over, and died of extreme fatigue. Whether he was an inexperienced bird or whether he had been weakened by his time spent in the basket aboard the sea-battered flying boat is not known. We do know that homing pigeons do not like to fly over water and will usually head for the nearest land, and thus often give themselves greater distances to cover, rather than fly a direct point-to-point course over water. In this case, however, the message carried one sentence that became the providence of the grim situation.

After three days and nights, when every available aircraft and surface vessel had kept in the trace pattern with no result, the Admiralty officials decided to abandon the search. But Lieutenant Commander B. S. Bannerman of H.M.S. *Halcyon*, a Royal Navy gunboat, refused to give up. "I want to justify the game little pigeon's flight. In that message Nicholl wrote 'May have missed Cromer,' and I have an idea they may have drifted well north of that point." (Cromer is on the Norfolk coast, about thirty miles north of Great Yarmouth.)

During the remaining hours of light that Friday, Bannerman steamed north and searched until darkness fell, but found no trace of the flying boat.

But what about 8666 out there on the angry North Sea? It was floundering hopelessly, taking water fast through a hole that had been made by an enemy shell fragment. Gasoline was running low and the flying boat was making little progress. The six men bailed endlessly, but a following sea constantly lifted their tail and rammed the hull nose in deep. Leckie had to turn north-northeast to keep afloat, but water entered fast and the men in the hull were up to their knees bailing like souls possessed.

Spindrift and weather soon put an end to their power and both propellers stopped turning. There was nothing left but to sit it out and hope. They drifted on, every man drenched to the skin. The crew had dreadful periods of seasickness, and as night crept on a gusty wind threatened to turn their leaking craft over. This continued until the starboard wing-tip float was wrenched away, when it was decided that someone would have to go out on the wing to add weight to level the floatless plane.

All through that night they took turns, lying out there in two-hour shifts, clinging to a strut while icy water swept over them every two or three minutes. That they were able to endure this trial is a tribute to their training and determination to survive. Leckie was so ill he ruptured a blood vessel and vomited blood. Trewin, who had been hauled aboard in an exhausted state, tried to make himself useful by handling the tiller while sitting in water up to his knees. They all were faint, weary, hungry, and thirsty, and finally they had to drink the rancid, rusty water that was drained from the engines' radiators.

Three days passed. It was now Saturday. The pale dawn drew its silver finger across the horizon, and in the strange half-light they were positive that as they looked about they could see the ghostly outlines of vessels. All sorts of ships, from drifters to light cruisers, seemed to be passing in review. It was difficult at times to tell if the vessels were coming or going, and then the distant forms faded and hope died as they realized that the broadening light was playing tricks — or had their tired eyes cheated them?

Then came the reward for their courage and endurance: at 10:30 A.M. a dim shape crept out of the mist and gradually took on outline, grew darker, and finally turned into a ship. Some men aboard it let out a rousing cheer but when the weary men in the hulk of 8666 tried to answer, their voices cracked and only a weak, broken croak responded.

It was Commander Bannerman of H.M.S. *Halcyon*, who, in tribute to a brave little pigeon, would not give up the search. The six weary airmen were hoisted aboard and made comfortable in the sick bay. Old 8666 was taken in tow, and eventually was returned to Great Yarmouth where she was put in the repair shed.

Squadron Commander Nicholl was up and about within two days; in fact, he went out on a routine patrol to make certain his nerves had not suffered. Three months later he was again in Number 8666, still searching for Zeppelins over Terschelling Island.

Meanwhile, in appreciation of the effort made by the pigeon that died after delivering its message, Nicholl had the bird stuffed and placed over the mantelpiece in the officers' mess. There is no name or number for that pigeon, but on a gold plate fixed to the wooden base Squadron Commander Nicholl had had engraved:

A Very Gallant Gentleman.

Thus did one hero honor another.

4 · · · Heroes With Wings

Shortly after the end of World War I, one of the most revered war memorials was erected at Edinburgh Castle in Scotland. Here can be seen plaques, statues, stained-glass windows, battle flags, and a beautifully illuminated Book of Remembrance that contains the name of every man and women who died in the service of the British Empire during that conflict. Also inserted in one wall is a stone on which is carved:

Remember the Beasts Who Served and Died.

Beneath this memorial are tablets to the dog, the horse, the camel, the ox, even to the canaries and the white mice that were taken into the trenches to detect poison gas, and last, but not least, a reproduction of three pigeons standing by their basket, about to spread their wings.

Among Great Britain's war birds who "served and died" was a young checkered hen with band N.U.2709

(National Union 2709), that flew from the trenches during the Battle of Menin in Belgium. She had only nine miles to go and the beating rain did not hamper her to any extent, yet just as she was nearing the area of her loft a German machine-gun bullet struck her and she lost speed, then floundered down into a morass of front-line mud. In order to regain her strength, the bird closed her eyes and lay all night in the continuing downpour. When an early morning sun warmed her she struggled into the air again and reached her loft with a very important message. That was all she could do, for she then fell, a handful of wet, blood-stained feathers, and before the loft man could open her capsule and retrieve the message, N.U.2709 was dead. This bird can still be seen in the United Services Museum in London as a reminder that a small pigeon can display the courage of a hero.

It is interesting to note that the British Royal Navy appreciated the value of carrier pigeons in certain emergencies and decided to put baskets of birds aboard all trawlers that were assigned to the dangerous task of minesweeping. At first the dour seamen of this service had little use for the idea, and in some cases the birds were neglected and often not fed for days. But during quiet spells the little birds won the men over, and they were treated at least as friendly mascots.

The day came, however, as they say in all stories, when Crisp, a red-checkered bird, was called upon. The trawler *Nelson* was attacked by a German U-boat, and the captain of the trawler, who was badly wounded by gunfire, crawled across his deck to the pigeon basket. Crisp was given a message and released.

The tale that follows justifies the belief that homing pigeons have the ability to find their home lofts, whether they are stationary or mobile. In this case, Crisp's home loft was aboard a pigeon ship that changed its moorings every few days, but this doughty little bird found the loft before night fell, and the news of the *Nelson's* plight was quickly relayed to a rescue force. The shot-up trawler was found and every sailor aboard was rescued. Needless to say, the homing pigeons in the trawler service were given preferential treatment from that time on.

When America entered World War I in 1917, our forces did not have one pigeon on their rolls. It seems that back in 1882 a Signal Corps expert had decided that "the use of pigeons in wartime is not practical." This was the same organization that pondered so long on the value of the military airplane.

From the minute he arrived in France, General Pershing faced a serious communications problem. In the first place, few Americans could speak French, and when the Signal Corps attempted to erect its own telephone system there were few men available who could handle the dual-language situation. A hurried call was sent home for American girls who could speak French, and in time that service improved considerably. Next, General Pershing saw how well the pigeon-courier service worked for the French and British, but he had no idea where he could get birds and loft men to fill this immediate demand. He sent another call home that resulted in the organization of a Pigeon Service. Thousands of birds were recruited from civilian pigeon fanciers, and many of them were sent over once they had been trained.

In order to fill the temporary gap the British contributed 600 birds from the British Pigeon Service, and it was this lot that had an important role in America's contribution to the victory. Cher Ami, one particular bird in this British donation, played the part that saved Major Whittlesey's Lost Battalion.

British Intelligence relied to a great extent on homing pigeons, particularly in the early days of the war. Shortly after the German Army invaded Belgium hundreds of birds were used in setting up a complete spy system, and some of them were called on to stage amazing tricks.

It is not always easy to establish an intelligence-agency ring in enemy-held territory, and for a time the British had to be satisfied with fake business offices in the Netherlands, where their agents could read German newspapers and periodicals and monitor German wireless communications. British agents also sought out and bought information from German deserters who, to avoid war, had scrambled through the barbed wire that separated the Netherlands from Belgium. One such deserter established contact with a British Intelligence agent and offered to sell him a book that contained full details of the German Army. In it was a complete list of every division, corps, and regiment, along with the names of all important commanders. To have tried to collect all this information, regiment by regiment, would have taken months of work. But the deserter, who had picked it up from some official German mail he had been transporting, had no idea of its real worth and, sold it to the British agent for less than $400. If he had held out, he could have got ten times that much. But such is the ill fortune of the renegade.

This lucky purchase was exceptional, for few of these deserter contacts were reliable, and a more businesslike system of gathering news direct from the heart of German operations had to be devised. Again homing pigeons were recruited, and again the little birds more than paid for their keep. Once more the blubbery balloon was called on to carry a basket of pigeons into German-held territory. Making the most of the prevailing winds and a time-clock device, the basket of birds would be released from the balloon and gently lowered to the ground by means of a parachute. A note in each basket requested the finder (presuming he would be a Belgian or a Frenchman) to use the message tubes, the lightweight paper — and the pigeons — to send back any news the finder might consider to be of importance to the Allies.

Early in the war most finders responded immediately, and in that way Allied Intelligence agents soon collected the names of a number of loyal men and women who were willing to work for the cause. For a time, too, much valuable information was reported. These winged messengers brought in such important intelligence that the Germans had to take steps to halt the practice, and signs were posted in every Belgian town that read in part:

It is learned that the enemy is dropping baskets containing homing pigeons in the hopes of getting military information.

Anyone finding one of these baskets must report it immediately to the military force.

Civilians are forbidden to open any of these baskets and any person disobeying this order will receive the severest punishment.

Any town hiding a homing pigeon will be fined 10,000 francs.

Pigeon espionage became so important that many innocent people were shot on evidence that a pigeon had been seen flying over their village. Anything remotely resembling a pigeon was shot down by German soldiers, who used shotguns or even machine guns, and eventually, in order to halt the sacrifice of Belgian civilians, homing pigeons were withdrawn from the Allied Intelligence service.

But before this decision was made the British often sent agents across the lines in piloted planes or in the baskets of free balloons that landed them in enemy territory. The balloons were sent off in the darkness on a favorable wind that carried them into enemy territory. Once a balloon reached its proposed landing area, the agent pulled the gas-release valve that permitted him to descend slowly. When he touched the ground he would hide or destroy the gasbag, then, carrying a basket of pigeons, he would move off into his working sector. Day by day, the little birds would carry his reports back, and when all of them had been released the agent would make his way into Switzerland, return to the Allied side of the line, and prepare for another such adventure.

Several variations of the pigeon-parachute idea were used to get birds to groups of soldiers who had been cut off behind the enemy lines. One arrangement had a basket of two, or four, pigeons that was carried across the lines by airplane and then released by a parachute in the area where it was known, or believed, that trapped soldiers were hidden. The basket, padded with straw, carried food for about two days and a pad and pencil. The marooned troops could then inform their superiors exactly where they were and what condition they were in, and offer suggestions for their rescue.

World War I revived interest in the value of homing pigeons, and nearly all European military forces took steps to augment the conventional training of the thousands of racing pigeons that were available to them in the lofts of fanciers everywhere.

Although speed had been an important adjunct in friendly competitions, the ability to get from point to point in the shortest possible time was not paramount. The peacetime bird had special training for club racing and had to become familiar with only two basic homes — his loft, and the travel basket in which he was transported from his home to the point of departure. All he carried was his own identification band and the rubber countermark used in the timing clock.

As soon as a homing pigeon was accepted for military

service he, as did his human counterpart, had to adjust to new and more difficult conditions. He had to learn to adapt to the message capsule, and in some instances to carry a tube with larger items, such as important photographic film, which was fitted to the center of his back.

The recruit had to learn to recognize a new loft, to live and move about in a mobile home, and to be handled by new men, week by week. When he was transported for message missions he might find himself aboard a trawler, a submarine, an airplane, or on the back of an infantryman. No matter where he went there was usually a violence of noise or movement. He might travel in an aircraft that was fired on from the ground — a terrifying experience — or his pilot might be set upon by an enemy airman, and the bewildered pigeon would be subjected to wild, evasive maneuvers, the like of which he had not experienced before.

The military service pigeon had to endure all these phases of training to prepare for the dangerous program ahead of him. Only thoroughbreds can stand this sort of work every day, and by the same token the men capable of giving this kind of training are a breed apart. They must be patient and enthusiastic, and have great affection for their charges. Most of the soldiers who were selected for this work were former peacetime fanciers, men who completely understood the task and the birds.

In military training the "squeakers" (as the birds are called until they are four to five weeks old) though not capable of flying and only just able to feed themselves, are placed on top of their lofts every day so that they can acquire a visual knowledge of the surrounding country. When they are eight weeks old they are allowed to fly for an hour at a time, twice a day, exercising in wide circles above their lofts. After a month of this routine, a program of basket-training is started in which they are taught to accept the uncomfortable accommodation and the bump and jostle of transportation from the lofts to liberation areas about five miles away. Most of the beginners return with little difficulty; they are just getting used to the variable surroundings. It is during this period of training that the birds that do not come up to the required standards are eliminated, and there always is a small percentage of these in each generation, even from the most blue-blooded parents.

According to British pigeon-training experts, the knowledge of local geography is of vital importance to homing pigeons. They dislike mountainous country at any time, possibly because wild birds of prey are to be encountered there, but, when necessary, they have to be encouraged to carry out their missions in such unfriendly sectors. Many wartime pigeons have a great aversion to flying over water and will instinctively make a wide detour if by so doing they can avoid the necessity of flying over a river, bay, or lake. Great care is therefore taken to teach military pigeons from earliest age to overcome this aversion, since the conservation of their strength is of paramount importance.

Weather conditions are another factor to which pigeons show a marked sensitiveness. In high winds or a drizzle the average homer flies as low as possible and will carry out his mission just skimming the trees or housetops, but on a fine day he will fly at an altitude of hundreds of feet. For this reason, enemy gunners had little trouble destroying these couriers in bad weather, a point to be remembered in connection with many of the incidents to be related here.

During the advanced military training the pigeons may be taken to areas ranging anywhere from ten to 125 miles from their lofts before they are released for the homeward journey. These distances are increased gradually by about 50 per cent over the length of the previous flight. It is in this period that the percentage of failures is highest, because the inherent quality known as the homing instinct, and the extent to which it can be developed, varies with each bird. A certain proportion will fail to regain their lofts, thus weeding themselves out as unsuitable for the precision required in military tasks. A few of these are given additional training to see if they will finally pass the rigid requirements.

Training along these lines continues until the bird is seven months old, during which time the program is broadened to include releases from various distances, in opposite directions, and problems in identification of the loft. Their final trials come when for the first time they are taken about fifty miles out to sea aboard a surface craft or an aircraft and released. They will then head straight for the land, and from that point try to reach their lofts in the shortest possible time.

A pigeon carrier, shown here in side and front views, accommodates one bird, a message book, leg capsules, and full directions for preparing the pigeon for flight.

Whether the pigeon has a built-in radar system that guides him home or whether he must be trained to use his homing instinct, it is generally accepted that the factors most likely to influence his rapid and safe return to his loft are the sun and the visibility. It is interesting to note that pigeons cannot be induced to fly in the dark unless they are very near home.

If darkness overtakes them while they are on a homeward flight, they will make for the nearest land, rest during the night, and complete the journey the next morning. There is no doubt that they fly fastest on fine days and show a distinct preference for clear weather.

Pigeons are not polygamous by instinct; and under ordinary conditions they will keep the same mate, and this fact can often be used to good advantage by the loft man. For instance, if a cock bird is released on a flight at a time when his mate is likely to be susceptible to the attentions of another male bird, he will fly home much faster than usual. So, wherever possible, the tasks given to birds are timed to coincide with their keenest condition, and in this case the eternal triangle achieves some useful purpose.

The trick of getting a returning bird to enter the loft trap quickly, and thus deliver its message as soon after arrival as possible, lies in the loft man's study and knowledge of each individual bird. Some pigeons will answer a familiar call or whistle; others will respond to the rattling of food in a can or pan; others will only enter on hearing the voice of a familiar keeper.

Aircrews and seamen aboard surface ships are warned that in the event of distress they must exercise great care to see that pigeons do not get wet before release. This is a factor likely to influence the bird's safe return to land. Once a pigeon's feathers become soggy, its wings lose their lift, and it cannot rise to any height or make much forward progress. The effort to remain airborne is so great that the task may prove to be beyond the pigeon's strength.

On the other hand, pigeons possess a remarkable vitality for their size, and their recuperative powers from injury or exhaustion are nothing short of extraordinary. A pigeon will recover from wounds the equivalent of which to a human being would be fatal. They often survive severe burns, broken legs, damaged wings, and similar extensive injuries. Given proper care and time to heal, they usually make a good recovery.

During World War II, a pigeon that completed more than 200 operational flights in bombers was seriously injured during an attack on Berlin. A shell fragment penetrated the aircraft and practically shot off the bird's beak. He was brought home, nursed, put on a special diet, and given three months' leave. During that time he grew a new beak, and was soon as frisky as ever.

On another occasion a homing pigeon was accidently dropped from an aircraft while still in its metal container. The box, with the bird in it, fell more than a hundred feet, and the impact on the ground was so violent the container was smashed, but beyond suffering a severe shaking that left it dazed momentarily, the pigeon emerged unharmed.

These military requirements, situations, and special training programs should be remembered in reading the various adventures experienced by these winged heroes.

5 ··· The Epic of Cher Ami

During the seventh day of the memorable Battle of the Argonne, the United States 77th Division (New York's Own) was the spearhead of the American attack. The 308th Regiment, which included a mixed battalion that was drawn from many units of the division, had moved forward more rapidly than the troops on its right and left, and was soon completely surrounded by the enemy. At the time this 308th became known as the "Lost Battalion," although practically everyone, including the Germans, knew where Major Charles W. Whittlesey's little force was huddling.

There has always been some debate as to whether Whittlesey's battalion had blundered into this trap or whether he had been ordered to advance as far as he could and take the calculated risk. Whatever the reason, this band of Americans was in a very dangerous situation. They could surrender, or they could dig in and make a stand, hoping that relieving forces would in time fight their way through to rescue them.

Major Whittlesey, a tall, spectacled New Englander, and a lawyer in peacetime, soon realized that unless he had a lot of luck his war career would be short and would contribute little to the hoped-for victory. His men had gotten into a pocket where the terrain was too thick with woods to permit accurate artillery support. Liaison with French forces on his left had been bad since the time he had started out, but more serious was the fact that his makeshift battalion was ill trained and badly equipped, and few of the men knew much about their weapons or how to use them under such circumstances.

Once he found that he was well ahead of his flank forces Major Whittlesey relayed his position to his superiors, who ordered him to "go ahead, pay no attention to flanks or losses." The New England major ordered his New York City boys to do just that, and they again floundered into a veritable hail of machine-gun fire. Whittlesey led his men to the right, and they crawled up Hill 198 until they came upon a portion of a deserted German trench line. He then encountered only occasional snipers and isolated machine-gun nests. Their main objective was a road that ran through the Charlevaux Valley, and it was this road that enticed them down from the security of the ridge. By the time he had taken over and settled down for the night with 679 men, Whittlesey discovered his plight, for the flanking forces of the 307th Regiment had gone astray, and he was completely on his own.

As he held on for the rest of that day (October 2, 1918) Major Whittlesey finally received a message from the commander of the 308th Regiment that read, "Do not advance until you receive the order from me." This order had been written at seven o'clock the night before and did not reach him until he was too far ahead to be helped by anyone. Fortunately, his Signals unit had a basket of pigeons, five birds, including one named Cher Ami which had been included in the British Army's donation to the American pigeon service.

Since he was hemmed in, Whittlesey might have considered fighting his way back to his original position between the American and French forces, but a general order had been issued that stated, "Ground once captured must not be given up in advance of direct orders." He did his best to advance, but by then the enemy had moved in to encircle the Americans. Occupying higher ground, and even cliffs, above the American positions, the Germans smothered the area with mortar and machine-gun fire. The battalion dug in, and fought back. Then Whittlesey sent out a pigeon with the message:

We are being shelled by German artillery. Can we not have artillery support?

All that afternoon of the second day a line of Germans advanced through the forest, hurling their famous potato-masher bombs, but as soon as they could be seen and identified, the Americans picked them off with rifles and machine guns. Whittlesey sent off another pigeon that carried the following appeal:

Situation very serious. Have not been able to re-establish runner posts. Need ammunition.

On the dawn of the third day, October 4, burial parties were as busy as the machine gunners. More German mortars lobbed shells into the Lost Battalion's area. Food was running short, and when their water gave out the only brook nearby was covered by German grenade throwers.

A third pigeon was released with the message: Our posts are broken, one runner captured. Germans in small numbers in our left rear. Have located German mortar and have sent platoon to get it. E Company met heavy resistance — at least 20 casualties.

The captured runner was Private Lowell R. Hollingshead, who, with several others, had tried to break out and go for relief and supplies. The small group was intercepted and most of it killed. Hollingshead however was only slightly wounded, and was taken before a German officer, Lieutenant Heinrich Prinz, who had once lived in the United States and spoke English well. While Hollingshead ate a warm prisoner-of-war meal, Lieutenant Prinz explained that it was inhumane for Hollingshead's commander to hold out in that pocket because there was no chance for escape. He suggested that Private Hollingshead return to his own lines carrying a message that suggested a humane surrender. After seeing the contents of the typewritten note, and after having his wound cared for, Hollingshead agreed to go back, carrying a white flag as he went, and deliver the note to his commanding officer.

The message read:

To the Commanding Officer — Infantry 77th Division.

Sir: — the bearer, Private Lowell R. Hollingshead, has been taken prisoner by us. He refused to give the German Intelligence officer any answer to his questions, and is quite an honorable fellow, doing honor to his Fatherland in the strictest sense of the word.

He has been charged against his will, believing that he is doing wrong to his country, to carry forward this present letter to the officer in charge of the battalion of the 77th Division, with the purpose to recommend this commander to surrender with his forces, as it would be quite useless to resist any more, in view of the present conditions.

The suffering of your wounded men can be heard over here in the German lines, and we are appealing to your humane sentiments to stop. A white flag shown by one of your men will tell us that you agree to these conditions. Please treat Private Lowell R. Hollingshead as an honorable man. He is quite a soldier. We envy you.

The German Commanding Officer.

Instead of surrendering as suggested, Major Whittlesey immediately removed a number of white marker strips that had been laid on the ground to show aircraft reconnaissance where to look for them, and in that act he eliminated all possibility of aid from the air. He then released another pigeon with the message:

> Germans are on cliff north of us and we have had to evacuate both flanks. Situation on left flank is very serious. Broke through two of our runner posts today. Casualties yesterday 8 killed, 80 wounded. In the same companies today, 1 killed, 60 wounded. Present effective strength of companies here 245.

The Yanks held on, although 434 of their strength had been cut down, when suddenly a new terror struck. American artillery began pounding shells into their battered sector. This was the most anxious period of the siege. Whittlesey, who was slightly wounded himself, huddled in a funk hole to write another emergency message. There were two pigeons left.

The man who cared for the pigeons was Sergeant Omar Richards, who, though he was by now exhausted and trembling with shell shock, crawled to the pigeon crate and withdrew one of the remaining birds. In his anxiety and weakness he fumbled the handling of the pigeon, and the homer fluttered away before the message could be inserted in the leg tube. Major Whittlesey stifled his impatience, and Sergeant Richards tried again, hauling out the last bird, known as Cher Ami.

The message read:

> We are along the road parallel 276.4. Our own artillery is dropping a barrage directly on us. For heaven's sake stop it!

Then came the most dramatic moment of the siege. Cher Ami rose in a tight spiral and circled the shelled area several times as more explosions roared below. Then, instead of coursing toward the 77th Division's lofts, he settled in a nearby tree and started to preen his feathers.

"Well I'll be . . ." Major Whittlesey snorted.

"Get out of there. You want them Germans to knock you off?" a soldier bellowed.

Cher Ami took no notice of the cries from below or the shelling from above; he continued to preen his feathers. After all, he had been cooped up in that dirty crate for days, and a soldier pigeon doesn't report in with an untidy appearance, does he?

Sergeant Richards finally risked his life by climbing the tree and sending Cher Ami on his way.

What happened from that time on can only be surmised. Being a pigeon Cher Ami could not talk, but once he started for his loft at Rampont twenty-five miles away he came under enemy fire. Shortly after leaving the tree he circled the area to pick up his direction, and a hissing slug from German machine-gun fire glanced along his head, taking out one eye.

Cher Ami staggered for a short time but soon bravely resumed his route. Artillery shrapnel and chunks of bursting shells screamed through the Argonne sky. One piece struck the bird's chest and broke his breastbone, and for a few seconds Cher Ami toppled toward the earth in a helpless spiral.

But he refused to give up, and, spreading his wings once more, he pulled out of his descent, fought back to his operating level, and hurried on. He had scarcely brought matters under control when another piece of shrapnel snapped one leg away, but fortunately the leg that bore the message tube was untouched and Cher Ami staggered into his loft at four o'clock in the afternoon.

At 4:15 the American barrage shelling stopped.

This brave little bird was awarded the *Croix de guerre* (French War Cross) for bravery, and several months later, after recovering from his injuries, he was returned home aboard the transport *Ohioan*. General Pershing saw to it personally that the hero pigeon crossed to his new home in America in a "pigeon-officer" cabin. Cher Ami became the pet of the Signal Corps headquarters in Washington, D. C., and, when he died, was suitably mounted and given an honored place in the Smithsonian Institution.

It would be gratifying to state that Cher Ami's heroic flight resulted in the rescue of the Lost Battalion, but in all fairness that honor goes to Private Abraham Krotoshinsky, Major Whittlesey's runner, who, after a harrowing experience, finally got through to headquarters of the 77th Division and returned with a rescue force that brought out the besieged Americans. Private Krotoshinsky was awarded the Distinguished Service Cross.

Another winged hero that would not give in to enemy gunfire was a large, powerful, black male bird named President Wilson. This particular homer was unusually speedy on all his missions. He began his military career while working with the early tank companies of that period — an experience that would have daunted many a bird, for the interior of a tank is as noisy and uncomfortable as the drum of a concrete mixer.

After a tour of duty with the early armored forces President Wilson was transferred to the Argonne sector, and on his second flight in this hazardous area he was sent off in a heavy fog to reach a loft located at Cuisy. This game bird was badly wounded during this epic flight, but eventually he made the trap, where he fell limp and exhausted. It was then discovered that one leg had been shot away and that he had been wounded in the chest, but the message was still safe and readable.

As soon as he could be removed from the pigeon hospital, President Wilson was sent back to the United States. He was a semi-invalid for years, and while housed at Fort Monmouth he had to be cooped with the hens because the other male birds would have taken advantage of his infirmity and pecked him to death. When he died in 1929 he also was mounted, and joined Cher Ami in the Smithsonian Institution.

Another male bird, one of disreputable appearance, was given the name of Spike. Bred in the United States and sent to France early in 1918, Spike had begun message carrying when he was only a few months old, and before he finished his service with the 77th Division he had carried fifty-two messages without suffering a scratch. On his return to Fort Monmouth he fathered several fine youngsters, among whom was Sunnybrook, who became a champion in the 1926 pigeon races. When Spike passed on at the age of seventeen, he left behind a lifetime companion named Mocker.

Mocker was a red cock, said to be the last of the war birds that served on the Western Front. He too had been bred in the United States, and, after being sent overseas he was soon in action in the Saint-Mihiel sector, where the Americans were attempting to break through the Hindenburg line. An enemy battery that was well camouflaged was playing havoc with our attacking forces. Taken on a dangerous patrol in which American scouts finally discovered the location of this weapon, Mocker was released, bearing a message that gave the exact position of the enemy fieldpiece.

This was another courageous flight, for Mocker was struck in the head by a piece of shrapnel. The wound destroyed one eye and streaked all his feathers with blood, but the enemy gun was silenced in twenty minutes.

Mocker was made of stern stuff, for despite his impaired sight he continued to fly war missions and before the Armistice was signed he had been wounded on two more occasions. However, he lived to be twenty-one years old — an age comparable to eighty years in a human — and sired a long list of sons and grandsons, all of whom signed on for military service at Fort Monmouth. Mocker also is mounted, and shares a shelf with Spike in the library at the Fort Monmouth base.

There were hundreds of other pigeon heroes in World War I, but only a few of them were given names. More than 90 per cent of the birds completed all of their missions successfully although they risked gunfire, barrage shellfire, and clouds of poison gas. Many were attacked and killed by the huge rats that infested the trenches and, as has been pointed out before, some were downed by enemy hawks. All of which proves that names are better remembered than numbers, for Cher Ami, President Wilson, Spike, and Mocker will never be forgotten.

The French Army and its Aviation Service made full use of courier pigeons very early in the war, and hundreds of baskets of these birds were borne to the lines aboard the historic auto-bus-and-taxi service that was set up to rush reservists to stem the tide at the First Battle of the Marne. Some reports have it that 25,000 pigeons were sent to the front, and nearly every unit had a few baskets stacked with their rations, ammunition, and entrenching tools. Regardless of his rank, any man who had a free hand was expected to carry a container of these feathered warriors.

A Captain Maitre of a unit of the 66th Marching Regiment was cut off for several days, and the plight of his company was such that unless help could be obtained his men would be killed or captured. His company had been in heavy action for weeks, and now the dreadful weather of March 1915 added to their misery. It was a grim question how long his weary force could hold out, so, putting all his trust in Blue Hen 3257-15, Captain Maitre sent off the following message to his colonel:

> The rain had made it impossible for our couriers to get through the lines. My soldiers have had nothing to drink for three days except the water from the shell holes. I have never been able to use my telephone. I ask for water, food, ammunition and more pigeons. Maitre.

The message was folded, rolled and inserted in the carrier tube, and 3257-15 was carefully released. She climbed fast in a tight circle through blustery rain that was turning to snow. Then, above the wild cry of the wind, the French heard the chatter of an enemy machine gun, and several high explosive shells overhead slammed their killing steel down on the trenches, but the blue hen finally turned and headed toward the headquarters of the 66th Regiment.

Half an hour later this gallant bird flopped into the headquarters loft, safely delivering the message. But as the loft attendant was removing the important paper he saw that Blue Hen 3257-15 had had both feet shot away, but that throughout the flight she had kept what was left of her message leg drawn up tight so that the capsule did not slide off and fall to the ground.

Another French bird, a gray cock numbered 902-15, had a broad band of white feathers that stretched across his back and along both wings. This marking was unusual, and when 902-15 was delivered to the 317th Marching Regiment the commanding officer, a Colonel Henry, stared at him in disgust and grumbled to his adjutant:

"Why do they even train a bird marked in that manner? Any fool would realize that that band of bright white feathers makes him an easy target for the enemy."

The adjutant rubbed his chin, and suggested, "Well, sir, let's keep him until the last. Things may get desperate enough, and, who knows, maybe he'll get through."

This proved to be a prophetic remark, for the regiment had desperate days; the enemy was strong and had plenty of field artillery, so that it was difficult to hold any position for very long. Finally the 317th made a move to get back to a fortified area in the town of Vandieres-sous-Châtillon. Most of these French soldiers were finally besieged in an old castle as the Germans swarmed about the area outside.

By dawn of July 16, 1916, although they were still holding out, the plight of the French was dreadful. The colonel sent out bird after bird with messages to the commander of the French 8th Division, asking for help and explaining their general situation. The messages were somewhat as follows:

6:45 A.M. Surrounded in castle and grounds. Please send provisions by airplane.

7:30 A.M. Have captured many prisoners. Need more food.

10:10 A.M. Completely surrounded but are holding on. Send ammunition and supplies.

Three birds were flown off, but none reached the headquarters of the 8th Division; apparently they had been shot down with bursts of machine-gun fire. No aid, no advice, no encouragement was received. At eleven o'clock Colonel Henry decided to risk the white-marked bird, 902-15, with a message that read:

Our own artillery is firing on us while the enemy is hard-pressing us with machine-gun fire. This is our last pigeon. Henry.

The bird was tossed free and, like an arrow, seemed to head instinctively for a small white cloud. He then disappeared, but a short time later he arrived at the division loft with his message. By early evening a detachment from the 8th Division fought its way in to relieve the besieged regiment. It was a thrilling rescue, one that was as much to the credit of the bird "with too many white feathers" as it was to the relief of the hard-pressed 317th Marching Regiment.

The city of Verdun and its fortified area surrounding it provided France's greatest glory in World War I. For five months the Germans threw in every available division, gun, airplane, and round of ammunition in an attempt to break through this defense and renew their drive toward Paris. The actual fighting front stretched over a distance of nearly fifteen miles — from Damloup to Avocourt — but the critical area was limited to the east bank of the Meuse river, where for seven weeks the compression of power and the concentration of artillery made the battlefield rock as if it were affected by an earthquake. No battle has surpassed Verdun in sheer horror, and few have equaled it. It was fought from late February in 1916 to the end of June that year.

The two renowned forts, Douaumont and Vaux, suffered the brunt of the enemy attack, and Vaux fell eventually on June 7. In this heroic defense, the French commander, known only as Commandant Raynal, held out in a classic resistance that won the admiration of the whole world.

When the German onrush started, Commandant Raynal had only 300 men in Fort Vaux. The fort was soon surrounded, and German artillery hammered the defense walls to rubble. A great number of courier pigeons were released to keep in touch with Verdun, but most of them were killed by machine-gun or shellfire. When trained dogs were tried out these intelligent animals were shot by rifle fire or died when the enemy for the first time used his Green-Cross (mustard) poison gas that was delivered by artillery shells.

This memorable effort by dogs and pigeons, which enabled Commandant Raynal to hold out until all supplies and drinking water had been consumed, was perpetuated by a monument that still stands in the city of Lille. It is a towering shaft with the figure of a woman holding a wounded pigeon to her shoulder. At the foot of the shaft is a marble tablet showing Commandant Raynal taking his last pigeon, a bird numbered 787-15, from a basket.

On the morning of June 6, 1916, exhausted, and with his men hungry and firing their last few rounds of ammunition, Commandant Raynal wrote a pathetic message:

> We are still holding out but must have help. We are under a devastating gas attack. This is my last pigeon. Raynal.

The bird survived the release through the blanket of poison gas, but before aid could be furnished Commandant Raynal had to surrender. Fort Vaux fell to the enemy, but its gallant commander was warmly received by the German Crown Prince Wilhelm in person, and congratulated for his stand. Number 787-15, who had made six message flights for his commandant, lived only a few days, its lungs having been seriously damaged by mustard gas. France awarded the brave bird the Legion of Honor.

The birds that were left to the Verdun defenders kept up their continued flights, enabling the Frenchmen to rally again and again with their famous cry, "They shall not pass!"

The great German push of March 1918 was a desperate effort to snatch victory from obvious defeat. The Allied High Command had had several indications that the enemy was about to make this supreme effort, but until the offensive actually jumped off it was difficult to know where the attack would take place. The Allies did know that the Germans had a fine network of railroads at their disposal, a transport system that permitted them to move great numbers of troops from one front to another. And to make the most of this network the Germans had set up areas of reserves that were gathered in strategic places from where they could be rushed to any prearranged point of attack.

Allied intelligence covered most of the enemy back areas, but it was particularly weak in the Grand Duchy of Luxembourg. Although holding warm sympathy for the French and Belgians the inhabitants were Teutonic in origin, and Allied agents had difficulty in setting up a worthwhile intelligence organization there. Because it was impossible to learn if the promised German offensive would strike out from that sector, the British decided to drop a man and a basket of pigeons by parachute in the area at night.

This was not an especially difficult trick; it had been successfully carried out on a number of occasions. The big problem was to find a man who would act as the agent. He had to be a Luxemburger who could speak the Low German dialect of the people; he had to know the country well, and have friends who would be willing to take the risk of hiding him in an emergency; and finally, he had to be willing to volunteer for the hazardous task. But the long arm of British Intelligence reached out and found a man who perfectly filled the bill.

He was a Major Steffen, a native Luxemburger who had spent much time in the Belgian Congo but by 1918 was a major in the British Army. He had proved himself in the field by winning the Distinguished Service Order.

Major Steffen had lived a full life, and at the outbreak of the war he had tried to enlist in the Belgian Army but was turned down. When he stated his case to the British they accepted him immediately, because they realized how much he could contribute to their Intelligence service. Steffen wished to be a real fighting man in the trenches, but he was too intelligent and imaginative to be used there and when the idea of his being dropped into Luxembourg for this dangerous mission was mentioned, he eagerly accepted.

Steffen had been of great value in questioning prisoners of war and was well grounded in the organization of the German Army. He could identify nearly every regimental or divisional insignia, and could figure out the various units that made up a typical German division. Because he knew the Grand Duchy territory well, it was hoped that he could complete his mission in a very short space of time, report on the number of troops concentrated there, and possibly even identify the divisions concerned.

He was old enough to realize the dangers of the trip: his airplane could be shot down while flying over enemy territory; if he bailed out safely there was a grim chance of being captured by an alert German sentry, which would mean immediate execution. He had no idea how close to his selected area the pilot would drop him. Even if he made a successful drop, he still had to dispose of the telltale parachute and find a place to hide the pigeons until he himself was properly established. When all these requirements had been filled, he had then to concentrate on gathering the information that was so urgently needed by the Allies.

He was given a pilot who had participated in several bombing raids in the Luxembourg area, a reliable man who knew the country well. Major Steffen received a short course in the use of the parachute — a rather primitive type that was devised from the pack used by kite-balloon observers. He was also introduced to his basket of pigeons and shown how to write concise messages and insert them in the message tubes the birds carried. Then Steffen, with the aid of a large-scale map, explained to his pilot exactly where he wished to be dropped. He planned to make for his father's house on the outskirts of Ettelbrück, in the central portion of the little country.

As night approached, when there was no moon, the British aircraft took off from a field near Albert, and the pilot had thus to cover a distance of 150 miles. After ninety minutes of flight, at a very high altitude to evade enemy antiaircraft fire, Steffen was advised that his destination lay below him, and clambering out of the restricted cockpit with the basket of twenty pigeons strapped to his chest, the major went over the side.

Everything went well; the parachute opened perfectly, and Steffen landed in an open field somewhat shaken but uninjured. He saw a hedge a short distance away and hid the parachute and the basket of pigeons there. He now wished that there was a moon, for he had to move in almost total darkness. He had a flashlight but dared not use it for fear of being spotted.

Once he had hidden the pigeons he cut across the field until he came to a macadam road, and after following it for about half a mile he reached a crossroads and a signpost. To his great relief he discovered that he was only twenty miles from Ettelbrück. He knew exactly where he was, where his father's home lay, and every road in the district. He returned to the field, retrieved his basket of pigeons, and started on the hazardous journey to his old home town.

Checking with his wrist watch he saw that it was already 10:30, but he felt that he had plenty of time to cover the necessary distance before daylight. That twenty-mile tramp must have been a terrifying experience both for the man and for the birds cooped in the restricted basket, but courier pigeons are accustomed to this discomfort and inconvenience. On several occasions Steffen had to dart into nearby hedges or ditches while approaching carts or groups of soldiers passed in the darkness. Had he been caught with the incriminating pigeons, all would have been lost.

It required all of Major Steffen's guile and courage to finish the trip in safety, and by the time he reached his father's house he was worn out and his nerves were stretched to shreds. But he had completed the twenty miles in five hours, and by 3:30 A.M. he was creeping up to the house he believed his father still occupied, although he had not heard from him in many months. He pondered on the possibility of German troops being quartered there, and then, risking all, he hid the pigeons once more, held on to a revolver in his coat pocket, and tapped on the window of what used to be his father's bedroom.

The window was raised immediately, and to his great relief a familiar grey head let out a muffled cry of astonishment. The elder Steffen recognized his son, and he was soon taken within the house.

Like his son, the elder Steffen was pro-Ally, but the major's mother was naturally concerned. Her anxious remonstrances were soon overcome, however, and a hiding place for the pigeons was found in the attic. In fact, two of them were immediately sent aloft with the news of Major Steffen's safe arrival.

The British agent knew that one of the great dangers he faced was the possibility of being recognized in his home district. Someone might remember him as the Luxemburger who had joined up with the British, so it was agreed that his father would cover the immediate district in the daytime and the major would work out as far as he could by night.

He had been well supplied with funds, and within a week he had ranged out over the whole of the Grand Duchy to gather in every speck of information. Three divisions were found to be at rest, a normal situation for this area, and the British agent assured his superiors that they need have no fears of heavy German concentrations moving into battle from that sector.

This, of course, was just negative information, but it

was important, and his messages, sent off three at a time for safety, reassured the British and French. An average of two out of every three birds sent out arrived. Once this critical situation was clarified, Major Steffen went into hiding in the city of Luxembourg where he remained until the Armistice. After the hostilities ceased, he rejoined the British Army and stayed on for several months, clearing up many other intelligence problems for history.

6···Heroes of World War II

Long ago, Nature imparted to birds the gift of flight that, combined with smooth efficiency and ease of motion, still mocks the finest man-made airplane.

The pigeon is an especially fine example of graceful flight, and, possessing as it does an acute sense of direction that surpasses that of any compass, it has been of considerable operational value in two world wars.

During World War II courier pigeons proved to be ideally suited for a twofold task. Not only were they carried in bomber aircraft for release in the event of the crew's having to force-land, but they were of great value as a means of rapid communication when normal channels had broken down, or when radio silence was imperative.

One black night when a heavy fog blanketed the North Sea, a British Beaufort bomber wallowed helplessly in the trough of heavy waves about 160 miles off the English coast. It had been on a very dangerous bombing mission and on its return had been disabled by a German Messerschmitt 109 fighter.

Once the bomber had been "ditched" and all crew members accounted for in the rubber dinghies, everyone realized that only by a great stroke of luck could they be picked up. As soon as the wrecked bomber went down their radio sets were denied them, but they did have the standard pigeon box that had been retrieved before the aircraft went under the waves. After scrawling an emergency message, the pilot carefully took out a grey-checkered cock and held him in the palm of his hand with his thumb over the bird's left shoulder and his forefinger on the right. The message was then rolled and inserted in the tube and the courier tossed free.

Every member of the crew knew that they were taking a large risk in releasing a pigeon after dark. In most instances the birds will seek out a ship mast or floating wreckage — anything on which to rest until daylight breaks. But a ditched bomber crew crowded into inflated rubber life rafts can survive only just so long. Bad weather, high seas, and their general physical condition all have a large part in their survival. In other words, the quicker the authorities ashore know that an aircraft is down, and the general location of it, the greater the hope of rescue.

This cock bird, however, evidently headed straight for his shore loft. He flew low, keeping the water in sight while the transparent third lid of his eyes flicked back and forth like a windshield wiper to keep the fog from blinding him. The checkered cock kept at his task for more than four hours, and once the shore line appeared he felt a new surge of vitality and his broad wings stroked rapidly to cover the last lap. Soaring higher, he searched for his home loft. Then, weary but still full of determination, he dropped down on his landing board and breasted his way through the trap door that led inside.

In a minute a pigeoneer had retrieved the message, which read,

> Landed helpless. Send motor launch — sea conditions getting worse.

The message included, of course, the general latitude and longitude figures of the bomber crew's position.

Because of this pigeon's effort, five British airmen were rescued from the sea and the enemy.

In March 1942, a British war pigeon named Winkie helped to rescue another Beaufort bomber crew, a tale that is still told whenever Royal Air Force men meet.

This particular Beaufort had been making an important reconnaissance patrol over the North Sea and along the Norwegian coast. This was the anxious time when a number of German pocket battleships were attempting to dash out of an occupied French port in the hope of breaking up the Allied North Atlantic convoy routes. Number 42 Squadron of Great Britain's Coastal Command, which was flying a torpedo-bomber version of the Beaufort, was assigned to this hazardous duty, and this particular plane, known as "M-for-Mother," was crewed by Squadron Leader W. H. Cliff, the pilot, Flying Officer McDonald, the navigator, Pilot Officer Tessier, the air gunner, and Sergeant Venn, the radio operator.

On February 12, 1942, the German warships *"Scharnhorst"* and *"Gneisenau"* slipped quietly out of the French seaport of Brest. They were joined by the *"Prinz Eugen"* and covered by a large screen of destroyers, minesweepers, and flak ships. By using the particularly bad weather, they were able to avoid British interception and to pass through the English Channel and head for the North Sea, from where they hoped to start a new program of naval destruction.

In the effort to trap these raider vessels, many torpedo-bomber and reconnaissance planes of the Royal Air Force were sent out, although the weather was malevolent. The Beaufort that was commanded by Squadron Leader Cliff was part of the British air armada, and their area of search was along the north coast of Denmark. Shortly after four o'clock in the afternoon, when their fuel was running low, Cliff called it a patrol and turned his nose back for Leuchars on the east coast of Scotland.

Once they were clear of the Skagerrak and well out over the North Sea again, the whole crew relaxed. The pilot plugged in his automatic pilot, and McDonald the navigator brought out a large flask of hot tea. Everyone but the radio sergeant felt his stomach muscles easing. In an hour or so another long, dangerous operation would be over.

Then the unexpected happened. They were taking their turns at the tea flask when suddenly everything went wrong. It was as if they had dropped into a giant concrete mixer. Smoke and flame poured from the port engine and, although the automatic pilot was in, the aircraft started diving for the ocean at terrific speed. Squadron Leader Cliff immediately cut out the automatic pilot and took over, but nothing he could do halted the crazy downward dive. The altimeter needle flipped past the 400-foot . . . the 300-foot . . . the 200-foot segments, and the next thing they knew they had piled into the icy water.

Squadron Leader Cliff was knocked out for a minute or so and when he came to he saw a yellow dinghy with Tessier and Venn safely aboard it. The commander got clear of the wreckage and started swimming toward the little lifeboat, and then he noticed that McDonald was heading in the same direction.

Once they were all in the dinghy they wondered what had happened to their plane. They had no idea, except that in some way one of the engines had exploded and set fire to the wing. When the aircraft hit the water the flames were doused, but it was too late then. They were down in the drink and miles from home.

As they were making themselves as comfortable as possible Squadron Leader Cliff saw that Sergeant Venn had remembered to save the basket of pigeons.

"Good heavens! How did you think of them?" he asked with true admiration.

And Venn said, "As soon as I knew we were in trouble

I sent out our call signal and an S.O.S. Then I clamped the key down and grabbed the pigeon basket. When I came to the surface I still had it, and here we are."

"Wonderful! Are they both all right?"

"No, sir. One of them either broke out during the crash or . . ."

"Which one is left . . . Winkie or Stinkie?"

"Stinkie, sir. Winkie must have gotten away."

"Impossible! No pigeon can fly far after getting as wet as he must have," Cliff grumbled. "We'll never hear of her again."

"Well, let's make the most of old Stinkie," McDonald suggested, and gave Cliff their estimated position.

Squadron Leader Cliff wrote a formal appeal for help, along with McDonald's latitude and longitude figures, inserted it in Stinkie's capsule, and carefully tossed up the bird for its release. But Stinkie wanted no part of a night flight. He acted as Cher Ami had done more than twenty-four years before. Instead of homing for Scotland, he circled twice and then returned to the dinghy.

"Go on. Get out of here!" Sergeant Venn yelled, and made a swipe at the bird.

Stinkie fluttered off and then returned again. Once he even pecked at Squadron Leader Cliff for being so inhospitable. As everyone lunged at or swung his arms at the pigeon, the dinghy almost capsized. but finally, realizing that he was not wanted, poor Stinkie circled once more and then reluctantly set course for home. The Beaufort crew watched him disappear into the darkening sky.

"I wonder how long it will take him," Tessier pondered.

"Those pigeons fly at about forty miles an hour," Mc-Donald explained. "The smart ones make full use of the winds and upward air currents. Old Stinkie ought to make it between three and four hours."

"Where's his loft?"

Sergeant Venn probed his memory. "I think those two came from a loft at Broughty Ferry (east Scotland). That's just north of the Tay, near Dundee. It's about the same distance from here to Leuchars. He'll make it all right."

"Wait a minute," Cliff said suddenly. "I seem to remember that pigeons won't fly at night. Is that right?"

Everyone else thought that such was the case.

As night settled down, the temperature lowered and occasional snow flurries hissed and needled their faces. A paring of moon appeared at times, and as they huddled together their imaginations played queer tricks. The dawn, however, brought stark reality. They hoped that if Stinkie had spent the night on the mast of some ship or on a chunk of floating wreckage, he would have started his flight for home by now.

Meanwhile the faint radio appeal that had been sent out by Sergeant Venn had been picked up at the base airfield, and the Operations staff was working out an area of sea to search with the first light of the next morning. Venn's hurried call signal had not been strong enough to give more than the vaguest indication of the position of the aircraft. It would be necessary to search an area of the North Sea nearly seventy miles square, in any part of which the dinghy might be found. To locate so tiny an object in such a large space would require a great deal of luck.

Just before dawn the next morning many aircraft started on a search. They had been in the air for less than an hour when the telephone in the Operations room tinkled. The controller answered it and learned that the caller was James Ross of 88 Long Lane, Broughty Ferry, who reported, "One of my pigeons which you were using has just come back all wet and oil-stained."

"Good! May we have the message, please?"

"There was no message on her, but I can give you her code number."

The controller checked the number in the pigeon records that were kept at the station and found that the bird (Winkie) had been in Squadron Leader Cliff's aircraft. It had been supplied from Mr. Ross's loft, and was one of a team of pigeons. Each team was carried in Coastal Command aircraft on every operational trip and released in emergencies.

The station navigator thought that by using a knowledge of the bird's "cruising speed," it might be possible to obtain a rough cross-check on the distance from land that it had been released.

Mr. Ross said that the bird would not fly at night and that in his opinion she had just managed to reach the coast of Scotland before it was dark. This narrowed the area of search by about half, and radio messages were sent to the several aircraft then over the sea, directing them to concentrate on the more likely area. Within twenty minutes, a crew of the Royal Netherlands Air Service in a Lockheed Hudson airplane found the dinghy just where the station navigator thought it might be, and radioed the position back to the base.

A spare dinghy, containing extra provisions and comforts, was dropped from the Hudson aircraft near the stranded men. Later that morning a Walrus (flying boat) alighted on the sea near them, and, although unable to pick them up because it had not sufficient accommodation, its crew assured the men from the Beaufort that they would soon be rescued. They also made certain that the Beaufort crew was well and cheerful.

That afternoon at two o'clock an R.A.F. high-speed launch took them on board. On the way back to the coast they heard how the pigeon had been instrumental in their rescue, but it was some time before they knew that it was Winkie, not Stinkie, who made the flight all the way back to Scotland.

Back at the loft, Winkie was given a special feed and her feathers were cleaned of the oil she had picked up when the aircraft crashed.

"She's a tough little bird," Mr. Ross said of her. He was a master plumber and a member of the National Pigeon Service. "She was Number 1 in the N.P.S. 1940 breed, and although she had been on a few training flights, this was what we would call her first operational trip. She must have plenty of stamina because she crossed about 100 miles of sea in a dirty, wet, cold condition. I have a lot of faith in her since she was one of the three survivors out of seventeen that the R.A.F. put through a number of rigorous tests. I am delighted that one of my birds should have done such a good job and I know it will be very heartening to pigeon fanciers all over the country who have offered their birds to the R.A.F."

Later on, to commemorate her part in the rescue of Squadron Leader Cliff's Beaufort crew, the station officials presented a plaque to Mr. Ross, which was engraved with an inscription expressing the squadron's thanks to the gallant little pigeon. Mr. Ross and Winkie were present during the ceremony and, while all the officers were saying most complimentary things about her, Winkie strutted up and down inside her basket, cooing her thanks. All the unfeathered guests raised their glasses and drank to the toast, "Good old Winkie."

In reply to the presentation of the plaque, Winkie's owner said, "I shall cherish this plaque more than any cup or trophy won by any of my pigeons, and I hope that Winkie's part in the rescue of Squadron Leader Cliff and his crew will increase the confidence of all airmen in the ability of these bird couriers to help them in these difficulties."

A special tankard was presented to the squadron of the Royal Netherlands Air Service in appreciation of the accurate navigation and skillful flying of the crew of the

Lockheed Hudson which had located the men from the Beaufort.

But in the end it was Winkie who gained the greatest award. She was given the British Dicken Award, which is considered the Victoria Cross of the war birds. She lived another eleven years, or until August 1953. She was then stuffed and put on view in the Dundee museum, just a few miles from her old loft at Broughty Ferry. In November 1953, Cliff, by then Wing Commander Cliff, D.S.O., appeared at the annual pigeon show in London to tell the story once more in aid of charity.

Venn and Tessier survived the war, but McDonald was killed in a Liberator on what was to have been his last operational patrol of the war. By a strange irony of fate the Liberator hit in almost exactly the same spot where McDonald had come down with Cliff and the others three and a half years earlier.

All these facts were obtained from the British Air Ministry's News Service.

Winkie was but one of tens of thousands of pigeons that were called to the colors by all nations fighting in World War II. Their numbers were so great that if they could have been flown in close formation, their wings would have darkened the skies, as did the flocks of wild pigeons that were seen in America less than a century ago.

But these war birds do not work in groups or squadrons. Each homing pigeon is expected to fly alone against the azure of the sky or the white of the clouds. He wears no

Charlie wears the Purple Heart he earned as a Signal Messenger for the Signal Company of the 90th Infantry Division in the Metz area during World War II.

uniform, only his code number and message tube. He bears no arms and may have to wing over a stormy sea from a plane or ship in distress. He may have to dart across a battlefield that is swept by artillery fire, or he may be released from an armored tank during a heavy ground attack — but he always flies alone.

How amazing when we consider the comparative size of a sixteen-ounce pigeon to a 125-millimeter gun, a block-buster bomb, a forty-ton tank, or a four-engined bomber! But it is their smallness that makes them so important in the communications systems. How important, may be noted in the fact that at the outbreak of the war in 1939 Great Britain rushed 14,000 of these war birds across the English Channel and the North Sea to aid her troops on all fronts.

As soon as this pigeon army had sailed away in their active-service baskets, the British War Office began to rid the British Isles of any Nazi pigeons — now considered to be spies that could fly to Germany with news of plane, ship, and troop movements. A million birds in British lofts were ordered to be released to fly outdoors. In this way, any that were owned by German agents in Great Britain would streak back to Germany, while the native (legal) birds would return to their home lofts.

Germany, however, tried an old trick. Paratroopers were flown over to England and, along with baskets of birds, were dropped in lonely spots where they would try to get in touch with Nazi sympathizers who could be counted on to do the agent's risky work. This spy system was uncovered when a passenger on a London train saw a man pull a pigeon from under his coat and toss it from a window. The passenger trailed this man when he left at the next station, and as a result the British Home Guard that was assigned to the duty of spotting paratroopers was doubled.

Then, too, peregrine hawks took a dreadful toll of Britain's war couriers, thereby "giving comfort to the enemy." Many of these birds were to be found on the Solway Cliffs on the northeast coast of England and for a time had a Roman holiday intercepting pigeons released by the Royal Air Force air crews. This was stopped when members of the Coast Guard found peregrine hawks' nests filled with pigeon skeletons and portions of aluminum capsules. To counter this, the local farmers kept up a hawk-shooting campaign for the rest of the war in order to eliminate these fierce birds of prey, which overtook and attacked with their knifelike talons all the war birds that flew in from the sea.

When Great Britain reached the zenith of her war production her pigeon army numbered almost 20,000 birds. When one reads of the many efforts made by these wartime couriers is it any wonder that the officers and men of the Pigeon Service were as proud of their lofts as was any captain of his ship or pilot of his plane?

7 · · · Wartime Pigeon Post

During the harrowing period between May and November of 1940, when it seemed that nothing would stop the German onrush to complete victory, 380 messages were sent from R.A.F. aircraft by courier pigeons. Three hundred and seven of these were safely delivered. Many of these messages were of a routine nature; not all of them could be considered in the vital S.O.S. category.

One of these messages brought news from Holland to England's East Midlands in just over four hours. In another exceptionally good performance, two pigeons that were released 340 miles from home and sent flying over a completely strange course made the flight in eleven hours. They had to cross two countries and a sea, but both of them arrived safely with their messages. One young pigeon delivered an S.O.S. message, after flying against a Channel gale and over 175 miles of sea, although it took him eight and one half hours of steady flying.

As pointed out before, pigeons are especially vulnerable to heavy rain, fog, or gales when flying over the sea. One bird, however, homed through from Norway in a winter blizzard. He arrived safely but died later of the strain.

In those days homing pigeons were under the control of the Signals Directorate of the Air Ministry. The section that was directly responsible was in charge of officers who were experts, men who had gained distinction in the sport of pigeon racing in peacetime and who also had a wide active-service experience.

Acting under the general direction of the Air Ministry was a committee of prominent racing-pigeon fanciers that organized the Racing Pigeon Service, and through this organization thousands of racing-pigeon fanciers put the services of their birds or their training skills at the disposal of their government.

The British National Pigeon Service volunteered to breed pigeons for the R.A.F. or the Army, and during the war supplied thousands of these birds. They used their own birds and lofts exclusively for message work for the services. It is interesting to note that their wives often helped in the labor entailed. These volunteers also assisted the local police or customs officers in various duties that involved pigeons.

It can be seen that the pigeon's task in World War II was somewhat different than that in the 1914–18 conflict, because of the greater speed and range of aircraft and the fact that the modern message form was enclosed in a message carrier and attached to the bird's leg *before* flight.

A white patch on the outside of the carrier enabled the position of the distress to be written in a few seconds at the moment of release. If there was more time, further information could be added.

In case a bird alighted on a ship, instructions for re-transmission were printed on the back of the S.O.S. form, which on many occasions saved much time.

During World War II most British bombers carried two pigeons in a special metal container. While on air missions, these birds were tended by airmen who were specially trained for the work. At each airfield where the birds were kept before their regular flights, they often were cared for by members of the Women's Auxiliary Air Force. By the end of the war many of the pigeons had run up amazing records of operational flying; one had flown 81 operational missions, another 73, and a third 64. A human birdman who had completed 30 missions, or a full tour of duty, usually felt that he was a real veteran.

Pigeons trained for war work have to go through a difficult period of flight instruction. For instance, they not only have to become acquainted and familiar with noise, altitude, and aerobatics experienced aboard the modern bomber, but they must learn how to leave an aircraft during flight. If it is necessary to release a bird with a special message while the aircraft is still airborne, the bird must have learned how to do a "dead drop" with his wings closed until he is well clear of the heavy slip stream of the propellers.

Young birds with little experience usually open their wings the instant they are put through the release hatch and are swept roughly away by the slip stream. Bewildered and ruffled, they usually take longer to set their courses and head for home. The old hands have learned to do the "dead drop" trick and avoid the violence of the propellers.

Pilots of the Royal Air Force generally spoke of bombing as "egg laying," but the first natural egg to be laid "while on active service" was the donation of a blue-checkered hen who during a fairly uneventful patrol — the kind often referred to as a "milk run" — made profitable use of her dull time in the basket. The egg was a beautiful white one, about the size of a crow's egg, and this happy event had been accomplished while the aircraft was patrolling the North Sea in the search for German U-boats.

Cooing contentedly, and quite unruffled by the journey, the proud bird and her egg were removed from the basket and taken to the pigeon house on the air station. The pigeon was granted indefinite leave and a second egg was produced. The blue-checkered hen and her mate, a slate-gray cock, kept the eggs warm, and probably anticipated the arrival of two ungainly squabs to feed and preen.

But duty to the service was more important than routine domesticity, and the day before the two eggs were hatched, the blue-checkered hen was called off the nest and sent on an important patrol. This time she was assigned to a long-range seaplane, a type that might be out on patrol for many hours. But duty was duty, and the blue-checkered

flier was soon well out over the North Sea. She no doubt
hoped that the slate-gray cock would hold the nest, so to
speak.

Toward twilight of this eventful day the big seaplane
was suddenly attacked by an enemy fighter, an aircraft
that carried six heavy-caliber guns. A burst of bullets
slammed through the wings and hull of the British airplane, and it went into a series of violent evasive tactics.
The pigeon basket was wrenched out of its holder, which
frightened and bewildered the two pigeons. Then the seaplane went into a steep glide and hit the sea with a crash.
Water rushed in, and the pigeon basket floated up and
down inside the half-submerged hull.

One of the crewmen finally retrieved the basket, and
the blue-checkered hen was withdrawn, provided with an
emergency message, and tossed free. She was soaked and
still dripping when released, but, possibly thinking of
home, her mate, and those two all-important eggs, she
bravely tried to rise. She worked hard to flip much of the
excess water from her feathers, and after a few minutes
of anxious endeavor finally reached dry upper air.

Ninety minutes later, almost like a ghost bird, the blue-
checkered hen dropped down out of a fog and found her
loft. The message was retrieved, and within twelve hours
a British destroyer had found and picked up the seaplane
crew.

The official R.A.F. report was, as usual, terse. All it
said was, "Sixty-three miles out on the North Sea a seaplane had successfully fought off a German fighter but

crashed in the sea with a dead engine — all aboard saved!"

There was nothing about the statement of one of the crewmen of the plane who said, "Blue-checkered hen, Number ----, although almost drowned, persisted in taking off and in spite of heavy mist flew sixty miles over the North Sea in ninety minutes."

It would have been more fitting if the R.A.F. had stated that this bird should be awarded the Victoria Cross, even if birds are not given military awards in Britain; but someone should have added that her pigeon-loft keeper knew from the sparkle in her bright-red eyes that what counted more to her was returning to her two little white eggs and her slate-gray mate.

But what does military bureaucracy know about domestic felicity?

When the remnants of the British Army were apparently trapped on the blood-soaked beaches of Dunkirk after the historic retreat, courier pigeons again played a memorable role.

Thousands of British Tommies who had refused to surrender were left helpless when France fell to the German Panzer onrush. They hung on for days, fighting rearguard actions to gain time, while formations of Stukas bombed them and fleets of Messerschmitts raked their ranks with burst after burst of machine-gun fire. While all this was going on hundreds of service pigeons were sent off with appeals for assistance. They braved the darting Me.109's and the screams of the attacking Stukas as they winged their way to their British lofts.

These feathered couriers brought appeals for boats — boats of any size, shape, or condition. The news of the plight of the Tommies spread from loft to loft in England, and every Britisher who had a boat or could handle anything that would float, risked his life trying to get across the Channel. In response to the messages carried by the pigeons, men who had never attempted to steer a boat set off in rowboats, power boats, fishing smacks, tugs, and yachts. Back and forth they sailed while the birds flew in with such messages as, "One hundred thousand still on the beaches!" . . . "Fifty thousand still hope for rescue" . . . "Only ten thousand left. Please help us!" Still the pigeons raced across the Channel and when the rescue was over more than 330,000 British and French troops had been evacuated, and saved to fight again. The last pigeon to be released carried General Lord Gort's memorable message: "All clear!"

But there was a tragic ending to the evacuation of Dunkirk. When the Germans heard how the British courier pigeons had played an important role, they ordered that every homing pigeon found in the occupied countries be put to death.

The first Allied attempt to return to the European continent was a mass Commando raid made by Canadian troops who had been stationed in England for many months. By the spring of 1942, when the first American troops were arriving in the British Isles, the Allied planners were being prodded by the Soviet demands for a second front. Such a move was impossible at the time, but it was agreed generally that some probing and test thrusts should be made — if only to learn the strength of the Germans in and around any of the numerous ports, harbors, and sea-front areas that continually threatened Great Britain.

One such probe selected from a number of French ports was Dieppe, a holiday town located at the mouth of the River Arques. It had been learned from air photographs that Dieppe was well defended by man and by the peculiar terrain. The town stands on high cliffs, which are mostly unscalable, broken here and there by narrow clefts or small rivers, the most important of which is the Arques, where the gap is approximately a mile in breadth, but the beaches at the foot of the cliffs are stony and inhospitable.

It is a mystery why this particular area was selected, as most successful amphibious operations are carried out against a sea front that has clear openings, easy progress inland, and as few natural obstacles as possible. The tide and water conditions at Dieppe are miserable. There are dangerous rocks in the sea bed, and the angle of the shore makes the task of beaching a landing craft a matter of great skill and luck. The clefts behind the beach are narrow, and could be easily wired and defended. And to add to all this, the Germans had erected heavy military opposition with 5.9 coast-defense guns at every likely landing place, so deployed that they could cover the main beach that paralleled the Dieppe promenade.

Although the area was carefully photographed from

the air, these inspections failed to disclose the full extent of the inland defenses; houses, hotels, and warehouses bristled with guns and temporary shelters. Any attempt to get ashore, even with tank support, faced a formidable defense fire from every direction. This foray, therefore, was doomed from the start, and whatever was learned of German practice, defense measures, or the enemy's determination to hang on to what he held was bought at a tremendous cost.

The Dieppe raid was principally a Canadian venture, but they had not been directly assigned to this dangerous mission; they had insisted on making the first thrust at the German-held mainland. Their commander, General Andrew G. L. McNaughton, had requested the task, pointing out that his men had been under arms for three years, and had too long been denied the opportunity of engaging the enemy. They had come to Britain with the expectation of fighting in France with the British Expeditionary Force, but instead had spent their time practicing military schemes and programs in the pastoral fields of southern England. General McNaughton said that every Canadian soldier had signed up to fight a savage Battle-of-Britain defense, and was charged with an intense desire to come face to face with the enemy.

The force left a number of English ports by moonrise on the evening of August 18–19, 1942, with the intention of being off the beachhead area just before dawn. All went well until a German tanker, which was being escorted by a number of armed trawlers, encountered the ships of the left flank. This gave the game away, as the trawlers started firing star shells that illuminated the sky, warning the land defenders to note — and take action. As a result, the Dieppe raid was doomed from the beginning.

Here again, courier pigeons had a part in the Canadian effort; as soon as the 5,000 raiders began their charge up the bullet-streaked beach, messages were sent back to the British base. It was imperative that radio silence be maintained early in the attack, and communications were limited to pigeon wings. Several of the birds that were sent up were immediately shot down by the heavy counterfire, but a white cock named Beachcomber was finally chosen to make the attempt. This bird paved the way, for he got through and set a splendid example, as over the next critical hour several more birds reached their British lofts, and plans were wisely put into action to withdraw the attacking troops.

Later on, when the Allies moved into North Africa to drive the famed Desert Fox, General Rommel, back across the Mediterranean, courier pigeons flew through clouds of desert sand and won new honors over the Libyan desert. When General Montgomery burst out of El Alamein, his tank force carried hundreds of pigeons that kept British armor in complete touch with troops and authorities in the rear. In these situations, they not only carried important messages, but special capsules that held small, hurriedly drawn maps explaining details of captured country, and warnings against mined roads.

The Germans, of course, also used homing pigeons in World War II. They had great coveys of highly trained birds that were cared for and housed in lofts set up along their own border. The chief central loft was in Berlin.

The officer-director in charge of German pigeon communications went the Allies one better when he devised a new means of using microfilm, by which he could send pages and pages of information, and even whole maps that had been photographically reduced and transferred to microfilm. To make certain that important messages got through, the microfilm was rolled into a loose tail feather that was tied among the matching feathers of a pigeon. When one of their courier birds was shot down, the microfilm would never be found — unless an Allied intelligence man knew where to look for it.

8 · · · America's War Birds

When the United States entered World War II, it was far better equipped with birds, trainers, and mobile lofts than it had been in 1917. As they had in Great Britain, civilian pigeon fanciers immediately contributed their flocks to the pigeon service of the United States Signal Corps, which soon added the additional training that was needed to turn these peacetime homers into war birds. The Signal Corps worked with great speed to live up to its motto of "Get the message through!"

Officers and men were quickly recruited to carry out this training and plan new strings of lofts. Suitable manuals teaching loft management, feeding, training, and breeding were written and distributed. Interestingly enough, many of the recruits who volunteered to serve in the pigeon service in World War II were the sons of fathers who had gone overseas in World War I to care for their winged couriers.

Hundreds of American pigeon fanciers joined up, one

of whom had bred 150 winners of noted long-distance races. This amateur volunteer was a very skilled bird sur-geon who had often sewn up the throats of courier pigeons torn by hawks, and he proved to be especially adept at setting the legs of birds wounded in action.

Although Fort Monmouth is remembered best as the chief base of the pigeon-training service, large flocks of birds were also trained at Fort Benning, Georgia, and at Fort Sam Houston, Texas. At Fort Monmouth, however, where more than twenty modern lofts were erected, the science was brought to its peak. It was here that great strides were made in teaching, or encouraging, pigeons to fly at night. The program consisted of short flights from nearby release areas, and this drill was increased week by week until most of the birds could be encouraged to carry out flights of fifty miles in complete darkness. Needless to say, such couriers were doubly useful in dire emergencies.

The experts at Fort Monmouth also worked for months to develop a bird that could make a two-way flight; that is to say, one who would bring a message from an advanced force to division headquarters, and then turn around and carry a reply back to the original senders. This accom-plishment was a military secret for some time, but we now know that these two-way fliers were fed at one place and given water at the other. Thus, a hungry pigeon that was sent off with a message for headquarters would eat his fill on arrival. Then when water was denied him, he would instinctively fly back from where he had come, knowing that water was available there. In the meantime, the base pigeoneer had inserted the reply to the original message, and the courier became a two-way operator.

One of the best-known birds that was capable of this type of flying was libelously called Mr. Corrigan after the famous Douglas ("Wrong Way") Corrigan, the aviator who in 1938 started a nonstop flight from Brooklyn to Los Angeles, but wound up in Dublin, Ireland, instead, with no passport, travel papers, or permission. In contrast, the homing pigeon named Mr. Corrigan was the fastest of his day. He was a great-great-great grandson of Always Faithful, a racer who had won a 750-mile classic between Chattanooga and Fort Monmouth, beating 1,000 other birds. Always Faithful, who certainly knew where he was going, covered the distance at almost a mile a minute.

The Fort Monmouth experts also developed a war bird that took photographs as it flew. This trick was accomplished with a light-weight camera actuated by slip stream, which took aerial photographs at stated intervals during flight. The aluminum camera was attached to the breast of a bird by simple elastic bands. A small force of trained birds could be sent out over the enemy lines to photograph moving troops, ammunition dumps, or any general activity under conditions that were impossible for military aircraft.

When birds were to be released from planes moving at high speed, someone in the American services developed a method to prevent the pigeons from being hurt in the stormlike slip stream. The bird was tossed clear in an ordinary grocery bag that had been slit on one side. Thus when the bird was released he fell clear, protected by the wrapper, but as soon as he was out of the turbulence the bag opened wide and blew away. The courier was then free to wing off on his mission. Another device overcame the effect of thin air at high altitude. If a bird was to be released at an altitude above 7,500 feet, the air was too thin to sustain him or his breathing while flying at full speed, so he was dropped free in a canvas-covered cage with an automatic timing device attached to it. This allowed the closed cage to fall to a more suitable atmosphere, and then the mechanism would open the cage and release the bird to fly in appropriate atmospheric pressure.

When there appeared to be a possibility that an enemy invasion might be attempted against the east coast areas of the United States, the Fort Monmouth pigeoneers worked on the problem of training birds for work in such a contingency. No one knew whether these birds, trained for field operations, would quickly adapt to conditions in metropolitan areas under fire. How would they react to being sent into large cities cluttered with skyscrapers, towering bridges, or the complexity of superhighways?

To find out, the Fort Monmouth officials brought a mobile loft to New York and parked it near the towering heights of Radio City. The birds were then taken out to nearby towns and set free. In all but two cases, these birds returned to Manhattan and skimmed through the great canyons between the skyscrapers and successfully sought out the loft. The two who failed, it was learned, had been intercepted by pigeon hawks hiding on the roof of a New York apartment.

Pigeons performed gallant and arduous service all through the Pacific campaign, when they must have saved the lives of thousands of Americans. During the terrible Battle of Guadalcanal, when mobile "walkie-talkie" radio equipment could not be used or infantry runners could not be sent through the dense undergrowth infested with Japanese snipers, courier pigeons were a godsend.

One American bird, Blackie Halligan, was sent off in the middle of a heavy skirmish when U.S. Marines were trying to fight their way out of a trap. Blackie was released with his emergency message. The bird had first to fight his way through the heavy foliage and treetops, and an enemy sniper who was armed with a .25-caliber rifle fired several shots at him. The brave Halligan was wounded but hung on, darted into the clear, and delivered his message, a flight that brought support and eventual rescue to hundreds of ambushed Marines.

Back in North Africa a gray hen named Lady Astor made a most thrilling flight during the early actions in French Morocco. Despite her name, Lady Astor was a native New Yorker who had been presented to the Signal Corps by a Manhattan pigeon club. On this particular occasion Lady Astor was sent on a flight of more than 90 miles with a message of great importance, but this brave little lady had what it takes, for she delivered her capsule intact although she arrived at her loft with three gaping wounds in her small body.

Her sergeant trainer looked at the wounded bird with sincere pride, saying, "If there were any medals for war birds, Lady Astor would sure get the finest."

Another American bird, suitably named Yank, made a memorable flight in North Africa. He was probably one of those characters who would not be outdone by any lady. This gray cock, who had been trained at Fort Benning, went to Tunisia by boat, train, and airplane, and after his familiarization period, and after getting accustomed to the Army's camouflaged loft, he was selected to fly back from the front with the first news that the Americans had captured Gafsa. He was released at a time that coincided with a wicked tropical storm, and had to fly through it for more than an hour and a half. How he ever reached American headquarters is one of the mysteries of homing-pigeon history.

Some of the pigeon stories that came out of North Africa seem fantastic. For instance, a blue-checkered cock, Wisconsin Boy, although only twelve weeks old, covered a 40-mile flight in exactly 40 minutes. He delivered a message reporting the distance of an American advance and the evacuation of Tébourba by the Germans. His home loft was located at Casablanca.

General Mark Clark still tells a classic story of three Army pigeons that had a major role when his Fifth Army was marching on Rome. This happened on November 8,

1943, when the Americans were pushing their way through the Apennines and slogging through ankle-deep mud, over narrow roads filled with land mines, booby traps, and deep shell holes.

An unnamed captain and a company of infantrymen were sent out on an advanced patrol to search out German positions that were tucked away on the commanding mountain slopes. Realizing the risks and hazards of such a patrol, the captain took along a crate of courier pigeons. It was well that he did so, for in a very short while the American H.Q. post received a pigeon message that read, "Surrounded on three sides." A short time later, however, a second bird brought the news, "Am attacking." Within an hour a third pigeon flew in bearing the message, "Have broken through."

Short, and to the point, but most satisfactory.

G.I. Joe is probably the best-remembered courier pigeon of World War II, because he did so much to sustain British-American courage and the spirit of comradeship. This well-known bird had served for many months with the American Fifth Army in Italy.

During the general advance a British brigade had moved with unexpected speed into the village of Colvi Vecchia near the Volturno river. Through some foul-up in communications their advance had not been relayed back to headquarters, and, in the belief that the Germans were still holding out there, the U.S. Army Air Force was ordered out in group strength to bomb the town. Everything was in order; planes were bombed-up, engines were running, and pilots and other crewmen were climbing into their planes.

Suddenly an order was flashed around the field.

"Hold it! A British brigade has fought its way into the town!"

G.I. Joe had had a rough time in getting clear of Colvi Vecchia, but, despite enemy artillery fire and heavy weather, he got through in time to head off the American bombing attack, a strike that unquestionably would have brought death to at least 1,000 British Tommies.

In closing this series of gallant flights, it might be well to include the number of the first American courier pigeon to be cited for bravery in World War II. This was U.S.1169, an Army bird loaned to the U.S. Coast Guard, and put aboard a schooner carrying out antisubmarine patrols far out in the Atlantic. A storm arose and developed into such a typhoon that the schooner was soon disabled and left floating helplessly with a broken-down radio.

In despair, knowing the strength of the winds, the sailors nevertheless released Number 1169 with a message and the exact location of the floundering ship. This pigeon fortunately got through to a Coast Guard station and help was rushed out immediately. Not only that, but the military command of the Chesapeake Bay sector made up a special honor for U.S.1169, a scroll that closed with "Keep 'em flying!"

By the middle of 1962 only three of the recognized

Army Signal Corps pigeon heroes of World War II were still alive. These select few were dispersed from Fort Monmouth when military pigeon training was closed down. They went to public zoos and similar institutions in the country.

Each of these hero birds had a record of at least twenty combat missions, and after the war was accommodated in a special Army shelter known as the Churchill Loft. These particular pigeons had excelled in heroic flights, carrying messages in North Africa, India-Burma, and Europe, and had written a special page in American military history.

Two of these hero pigeons, still alive and apparently in excellent condition, are Caesar and Flipper, who at this writing are to be seen at the Oak Park Zoo in Montgomery, Alabama. Another living hero bird is Geronimo, now housed in Woodland Park Zoological Gardens in Seattle, Washington. This courier carried out thirty combat flights.

Caesar, a topflight hero, is credited with forty-four combat flights in North Africa, and also with a 300-mile flight, crossing the Mediterranean with an important message for American troops in Tunisia. Flipper is a combat veteran with twenty missions in Europe.

G.I. Joe, the bird credited with saving the lives of 1,000 British troops, died June 3, 1961. Before he passed on he was awarded the Dicken Medal by the Lord Mayor of London. G.I. Joe died at the Detroit Zoological Gardens, to which he had been presented by the Army along with another hero bird, named C.O.D.

C.O.D. had flown twenty combat missions in the Mediterranean theater of war, but he died on April 26, 1957, shortly after his arrival in Detroit.

Eureka, who went with Geronimo to Seattle, died November 26, 1961. He, too, was credited with twenty missions.

Two Ohio sites were the recent homes of four more courier heroes. The Dayton Museum of Natural History was presented with Lady Karen and Special Delivery, and the Cleveland Zoological Gardens in Brookside Park were honored with Pro Patria and Crossed Flags. Lady Karen, who died early in 1961, had flown thirty-one missions, and Special Delivery made more than twenty flights. Both birds put in their war time in Italy. Special Delivery died November 19, 1961. Pro Patria was credited with thirty-five combat flights, and Crossed Flags with twenty. The former bird died October 18, 1961, the latter on April 27, 1957.

The National Zoological Park in Washington, D.C., housed Anzio Boy and Global Girl. Anzio Boy completed thirty-eight wartime missions in Italy, and Global Girl delivered twenty-three messages over far-flung areas in the Mediterranean theater. Anzio Boy died December 3, 1958, and Global Girl on October 22, 1959.

The Baltimore Zoo in Druid Hill Park, Baltimore, Maryland, received Yank and Apex. Yank, who died on May 24, 1959, will be remembered for carrying the message that reported the fall of Gafsa in Tunisia. He was also the bearer of an urgent message for the late General

George S. Patton, Jr., making the hazardous flight of 90 miles in 100 minutes. Apex, with more than twenty combat missions in the India-Burma theater of operations, died October 15, 1957.

Scoop, another hero with a record of twenty combat missions, for American troops in Algiers, went to Riverside Park Zoo in Scotts Bluff, Nebraska. He died late in 1959.

Index

The Author

ARCH WHITEHOUSE is a veteran of World War I, and has written several books about the famous men and events of that period.

Born in England, Whitehouse came to the United States when he was nine years old. He returned to England to join the Royal Flying Corps during World War I, and flew a single-seater fighter plane. In World War II he was a war correspondent, successively with the Royal Canadian Air Force, the U.S. Navy, and finally the U.S. Army Air Corps in Europe.

Author of some fifteen books, including two in the Putnam LIVES TO REMEMBER series, *Billy Mitchell* and *John J. Pershing*, Mr. Whitehouse also writes frequently for national magazines. He and his wife now live in Montvale, New Jersey.